Attacks on the Press

The Committee to Protect Journalists is an independent, nonprofit organization that promotes press freedom worldwide, defending the right of journalists to report the news without fear of reprisal. CPJ ensures the free flow of news and commentary by taking action wherever journalists are attacked, imprisoned, killed, kidnapped, threatened, censored or harassed.

Attacks on the Press

2016 EDITION

Gender and Media Freedom Worldwide

Committee to Protect Journalists

WILEY | Bloomberg
PRESS

Editor: Alan Huffman
Editorial Director: Elana Beiser
Copy Editor: April Simpson

Cover photo: Jordan TV journalist Nepal Farsakh reacts after Israeli security forces spray her face with pepper gas on July 2, 2015, as she was covering a demonstration by Palestinians on a road leading to the Adam settlement, near the West Bank village of Jabba. (Abbas Momani, AFP/Courtesy of Getty Images)

Cover design: © Committee to Protect Journalists
© 2016 Committee to Protect Journalists, New York. All rights reserved.
Published by John Wiley & Sons, Inc., Hoboken, New Jersey.
The first edition of *Attacks on the Press* was published by Bloomberg Press in 2013.
Published simultaneously in Canada.

For general information on our other products and services or for technical support, please contact our Customer Care Department within the United States at (800) 762-2974, outside the United States at (317) 572-3993 or fax (317) 572-4002.

Wiley publishes in a variety of print and electronic formats and by print-on-demand. Some material included with standard print versions of this book may not be included in e-books or in print-on-demand. If this book refers to media such as a CD or DVD that is not included in the version you purchased, you may download this material at http://booksupport.wiley.com. For more information about Wiley products, visit www.wiley.com.

Library of Congress Cataloging-in-Publication Data:

ISBN 978-1-119-23090-8 (Paperback)
ISBN 978-1-119-23091-5 (ePDF)
ISBN 978-1-119-23094-6 (ePub)

Printed in the United States of America.

10 9 8 7 6 5 4 3 2 1

FSC
www.fsc.org
MIX
Paper from
responsible sources
FSC® C101537

Contents

Introduction
Breaking the Silence

By Joel Simon

An Egyptian youth grabs a woman crossing the street with her friends
in Cairo in 2012. Several female journalists were attacked in the city's
Tahrir Square after the fall of Hosni Mubarak.

Source: AP/Ahmed Abdelatif, *El Shorouk Newspaper*

O n February 11, 2011, as journalists were documenting the raucous celebration in Cairo's Tahrir Square following the fall of Hosni Mubarak, the story took a sudden and unexpected turn. CBS 60 Minutes correspondent Lara Logan, who was reporting from the square, was violently separated from her crew and security detail by a mob of men. They tore her clothes from her body, beat her and brutalized her while repeatedly raping her with their hands. Logan was saved by a group of Egyptian women who berated her attackers until a group of Egyptian army officers arrived and took her to safety.

Details of the attack on Logan were sketchy, and in the immediate aftermath there was a good deal of confusion and some predictable but unfortunate criticism as well. Some raised questions about Logan's judgment in reporting from Tahrir Square at a volatile moment. Others questioned the appropriateness of her dress.

But there was a more serious concern among leading female journalists with whom I was in touch at the time. They worried that the intensive coverage of Logan's attack could affect them professionally. These journalists had throughout their careers overcome discrimination and resistance from editors and managers in taking on the most dangerous and difficult assignments. They worried that a focus on the risk of sexualized violence would reinforce resistance from editors. The concern was not entirely academic. In November 2011, after a sexualized attack on a French journalist, Caroline Sinz, Reporters Without Borders (RSF) issued a statement noting, "This is at least the third time a woman reporter has been sexually assaulted since the start of the Egyptian revolution. Media should take this into account and for the time being stop sending female journalists to cover the situation in Egypt."

The response was immediate and fierce. Writing in the *Guardian*,[1] journalist and documentary filmmaker Jenny Kleeman noted, "The threat to women is undeniable and should not be underestimated. But then again, so is the threat to men. In 2011 so far, 58 journalists have been killed on the job, only two of them female. Yet I see no statement from RSF urging men not to be sent into the field." In response to the outcry, RSF modified its statement, which today reads, "It is more dangerous for a woman than a man to cover the demonstrations in Tahrir Square. That is the reality and the media must face it."[2]

At CPJ, we faced criticism of our own. Many friends of the organization pointed out that we had not done enough to document sexualized violence and that we did not collect the kind of comprehensive data we have on killed and imprisoned journalists. Of course, it is more difficult to document sexualized violence because of its stigmatizing nature, but our then-senior editor, Lauren Wolfe, demonstrated that it could be done through persistence and determination.

During the three months following the attack on Logan, Wolfe interviewed dozens of reporters, who described their experience with sexualized violence, many speaking publicly for the first time. These incidents ranged from rape to groping and harassment during demonstrations. Victims told Wolfe that they had not spoken out for a variety of reasons, including societal norms, a belief that authorities would not pursue an investigation, and, most distressingly, a concern that they would face discrimination in their own newsrooms.

The CPJ report was dubbed "The Silencing Crime,"[3] a reference to the way that sexualized violence both stigmatizes and censors. "The Silencing Crime" garnered intensive media coverage, and was the first in a series of reports, including a combined effort from the International News Safety Institute (INSI) and the International Women's Media Foundation (IWMF), which in March 2014 published "Violence and Harassment Against Women in the News Media: A Global Picture."[4]

On May 1, 2011, Logan was interviewed on "60 Minutes"[5] by her colleague Scott Pelley and described her experience in unflinching detail. When asked why she was speaking out, Logan said she wanted to "break the silence," noting that women "never complain about incidents of sexual violence because you don't want someone to say, 'Well, women shouldn't be out there.' But I think there are a lot of women who experience these kinds of things as journalists and they don't want it to stop their job because they do it for the same reasons as me—they are committed to what they do. They are not adrenaline junkies, you know, they're not glory hounds, they do it because they believe in being journalists."

■ ■ ■

Five years later, the landscape looks very different. It's better in some ways, but worse in others. This year, *Attacks on the Press* looks not only at sexualized violence and online harassment but also more broadly at the intersection of gender and press freedom from a variety of perspectives.

Colombian journalist Jineth Bedoya Lima provides a harrowing and moving account of being raped 16 years ago by men who sought to punish her for her reporting on arms trafficking and to terrorize others who might pursue similar stories. Bedoya would not be silenced. Not only did she continue to speak out, but also her courage rallied the nation of Colombia to confront the issue of sexualized violence. Today, by presidential decree, the date of Bedoya's abduction, May 25, is marked with marches and rallies as the National Day for the Dignity of Women Victims of Sexual Violence. "Words can indeed change the world," notes Bedoya in her essay.

Words can also do tremendous harm, as we see in a series of essays about the online harassment of women journalists, including the phenomenon of Internet trolling—the systematic targeting of online posters by hostile individuals, which in many cases includes threats of physical harm. In her fascinating reported piece, Elisabeth Witchel explores the issue from the perspective of the trolls. Who are these people, and why do they do what they do? The answers are surprising.

A piece by Michelle Ferrier, a former columnist for Florida's *Daytona Beach News-Journal*, describes the emotional toll inflicted by relentless denigration and verbal assault. In Ferrier's case, most of the attacks came in the form of letters and not tweets, and focused more on her race than her gender. But Ferrier captures the feelings of fear, helplessness and isolation of those experiencing unceasing insults. "Unless it has happened to you, it is hard to imagine what this kind of stalking feels like," she writes. "Trust me. You don't want to know."

Other essays examine the challenge and consequences of gender-based discrimination in a variety of societies. Yaqiu Wang describes how even as more and more women in China enter the field of journalism, their opportunities for advancement remain limited. Preethi Nallu looks at female journalists reporting on post-Qaddafi Libya, which has become less overtly repressive but more polarized and violent. Some female journalists have gone into exile due to their high visibility. Jessica Jerreat examines the varying challenges faced by transgender journalists overcoming discrimination in newsrooms in the U.K. and staying safe while reporting in Uganda. Jake Naughton explores how gay men and women—and even reporters who cover their issues—are subject to harassment in Kenya.

Meanwhile, Alessandria Masi and Erin Banco describe the advantages that female journalists bring to the coverage of complex stories, reminding us of what is lost when their voices are shut out. Masi, a journalist based in Beirut, uses social media to report on the Islamic State, finding that her gender gives her new insights into their recruitment strategies and the kind of society they are seeking to create. Banco, who reported from the Middle East region, reveals how she gained experience as a conflict reporter but had to earn the respect of her male sources and colleagues. At the same time, she found her gender to be an advantage. "As a woman, I am able to gain access to the women and girls, who are often asked to sit in a side room while I interview their father, brother or uncle," she writes. "As a woman, I can sit with a mother and her children alone without her husband and speak to her candidly." Sometimes, notes Kathleen Carroll in her essay, a woman may also be granted special access when it comes to comforting journalists who suffer attacks.

There are plenty of inspiring stories, although sometimes you have to look to find them. Arzu Geybullayeva describes how her friend, Azerbaijani journalist Khadija Ismayilova, has courageously defied all efforts to silence her, standing up to smear campaigns, character assassination and, ultimately, a bogus prosecution and trial that resulted in her being sentenced to seven and a half years in prison. Kerry Paterson describes how journalists are helping bring justice to victims of sexual violence—sometimes at the hands of peacekeepers—in the Democratic Republic of Congo and the Central African Republic. And María Salazar-Ferro profiles four courageous women who have led the fight for justice for journalists who have gone missing or been imprisoned or killed.

■ ■ ■

The essays in this volume challenge the various ways in which gender affects what we know about the world, and in particular the challenges women face in all societies to bring us the news. A number of other essays tackle the difficult question of what can be done.

CPJ's advocacy director, Courtney Radsch, considers the ways journalists are attempting to combat gender-based online abuse and the debate over online anonymity. Karen Coates looks at some of the specialized safety training being provided to female journalists. Dunja Mijatović, the special rapporteur for Freedom of Expression of the OSCE, outlines a series of practical and concrete steps that policymakers can take to combat online harassment.

These are all important measures that have the potential to improve the lives of journalists of any gender, and particularly women. But given the scope of the challenges—sexualized violence, harassment, discrimination—they seem distinctly unsatisfying. Clearly, vital voices are being suppressed and, as a result, some of the information we need to make sense of a complex world is missing.

This is terribly distressing until one considers the extent to which the open discussion of the issue of gender represents progress. Only a few years ago, when Lauren Wolfe was researching her report for CPJ, she found so many journalists who had never talked about their experiences. Today, the environment has begun to change. As this volume makes clear, victims of sexualized violence—mostly women, but men as well—are speaking out. By doing so, they are helping reduce the stigma, making it easier for other victims to discuss their experiences. This, in turn, helps forge responses.

As more journalists speak out about these hidden abuses, CPJ is better able to document the violations. This means more data that will help us understand the nature and scope of the problem. In 2016, CPJ will make a more concerted effort to document incidents of sexualized violence and tag them on our website. We will also be speaking out more, using this book to organize a series of events and discussions.

Sexualized violence is different. At its most extreme, it is an almost incomprehensible horror, as Jineth Bedoya Lima's account makes clear. It can never be normalized or accepted. But journalists must confront the risk in order to do their work. Editors, managers, colleagues and press freedom advocates must honor and support their decisions, seeking to mitigate the risk while recognizing it can never be eliminated. The reality of sexualized violence—not to mention the other challenges that women face in bringing us the news—should never be used to limit opportunities. Though solutions are hard to come by, talking openly is an important first step. We hope this book makes a contribution to that difficult process.

■ ■ ■

Joel Simon *is the executive director of the Committee to Protect Journalists. He has written widely on media issues, contributing to* Slate, Columbia Journalism Review, The New York Review of Books, World Policy Journal, Asahi Shimbun *and* The Times of India. *His book,* The New Censorship: Inside the Global Battle for Media Freedom, *was published in November 2014.*

1. The Sadness of May the 25th

By Jineth Bedoya Lima

Translated from Spanish by Wilson Vega

After being kidnapped and raped, Jineth Bedoya Lima considered suicide or exile. Instead, she chose to continue working as a journalist in Colombia.

Source: Abel Cardenas/ *El Tiempo*

To rewrite one's story, when it is so painful, feels like a kind of suicide. Psychologists would say that is part of a grieving process, helping close nefarious chapters in life. We, the victims of sexual violence, are often told that. But I think it would be more helpful to the goal of moving forward if receiving justice were part of the process.

My last 15 years and six months have been a mixture of pain, anger, infinite love for my work, obstinacy and, yes, hopelessness. I have tried to be patient and willing since that day, May 25, 2000, when I was kidnapped[1] at the gates of La Modelo prison in Bogotá. My patient deliberation has led me to recognize myself as a victim, then as a survivor and now as an activist defending the rights of women. Though my patience has not overcome the entanglement of my case in the cobwebs of oblivion, it has given me the strength to not falter while continuing to live and work.

In 2010, I published a book, *I Speak to You from the Prison*, which is a small collection of stories about men and women in Colombian jails. There is a part of my own story in the book, because on the day that I was kidnapped at La Modelo, I lost my most precious freedom. It was the freedom to dream.

At the time, I was a young writer in Bogotá who wanted to swallow the world. I didn't care if I slept only two hours at night or ate once a day. I cared only about walking the cold floors of Paloquemao, Bogotá's biggest court complex, to hear the news of the city's latest crimes, or entering the infernal La Modelo to research stories for the pages of the newspaper *El Espectador*.

The La Modelo prison was considered one of the most dangerous in the world, overcrowded to an unbelievable 197 percent of its capacity. The prisoners slept on top of each other and the biggest criminal enterprises in the country—arms trafficking, kidnapping, forced disappearance, drug trafficking and extortion—were centered there.

During my visits to La Modelo, in addition to the human drama, I crashed head-on into the corrupt and indiscriminate reality of arms trafficking and kidnapping. The prison's large criminal network was being directed under the auspices of high officials of the security forces (the police and the army), though at that time I had no idea this was the case. Now that I see it clearly, there is no room for regret over what I should not have done—or rather, what I should have never investigated. There is no turning back the clock.

I believed that my stories were changing the world. But the criminals who kidnapped me were the actors in a plan to shut me up. My audacity to mess with that criminal web almost cost me my life, and left a deep wound that today, 15 years later, is far from closed.

Journalists are accustomed to writing the stories of others, which may make it harder for us to write our own. I was raped during my kidnapping, and one day I was asked in an interview what it was like and if I could recount it. So I decided to write about it, to go back to my pain and tragedy without allowing it to become a tabloid episode. The problem is that we journalists often believe we have no right to make our feelings public.

The arms trafficking network I discovered inside La Modelo was an empire of unimaginable size and complexity. Within it, I found terrible scenes of displaced women, partners of both paramilitaries and guerrillas, even simple visitors who were sexually abused. It was another outcropping of Colombia's decay, though for me it was very far from everyday life.

But that journalistic work proved to be costly, and led to retaliation because I touched the wrong person. On that May morning, I came to the door of La Modelo looking for an interview with a paramilitary figure and ended up drugged and gagged in the back of a truck heading to hell.

At first, I did not understand what was happening. I thought they had been ordered by Carlos Castaño, the top leader of the Autodefensas Unidas de Colombia (a paramilitary and drug trafficking group), to ask me why I was publishing so many stories about him, or why I had revealed this network of arms trafficking within the prison, in complicity with some members of the National Police and the National Institute of Corrections.

I speculated, in a whirlwind of thoughts and ideas about what was happening, while I was choking on my own vomit. I was dizzy, and when I begged them to let me throw up, they put a tape on my mouth. When I tried to remove the band covering my eyes, I got a kick in the face.

Until then, I thought it was only a beating as a warning, that it would soon be over and I would be able to breathe. But then the truck stopped in an open field where there were many men.

A few minutes passed and again the subject who had pointed a gun at me at the doors of the jail, the one who had kicked me in the face and had torn strands of my hair while shaking my head, was back. For the umpteenth time, he put his gun to my temple, loaded it and, after hitting me, made me open my eyes as much as I was able. "Look really well at my face, you S.O.B.," he said. "Look at it because you will never forget it."

I felt an icy cold throughout my body and fear hit me in the chest. I tried every possible way to stop them from ripping my pants and underwear. I tried to gather all possible strength to make sure they didn't touch me or come closer to my body, but his other cronies only further plunged me into humiliation. I was only 26 years old and my life had just been shattered by three criminals. They almost broke my left arm and left me with a hematoma from the fingertip to the collarbone. A few hours after the torture, beatings and outrage, they left me abandoned on a highway, on the road to Puerto López, Meta, three hours from Bogotá.

I wanted to die.

After receiving the help of a taxi driver and being transferred to a clinic, I began to face the disgraceful reality that awaited me. While suffering the examination of forensic medicine, which is really a second rape, I questioned if maybe the fault had been mine. Unfortunately, women who are raped often think that way. Did I wear the wrong blouse? Was it the skirt? Were my clothes showing more than they should? It took me many months to stop feeling filthy and many years to allow a man to touch me again. Such a violation is not like a fist or a blow; it is a crime that destroys our lives.

The second part of the nightmare came as I debated my next reality: whether to commit suicide or go into exile. In the end, I chose neither. I chose to continue doing journalism in Colombia.

I still do not know where I found the strength to return to the newsroom, to my notes and to my tape recorder. What I do see clearly is what motivated me. I understand now that my love for this profession and for my work as a reporter was greater than the pain of my body and my soul.

It is not easy to write about the Colombian conflict when you know that part of your personal story is recounted daily in the stories of the protagonists of your chronicles, but almost recklessly, I returned to the line of fire. For years, I documented the confrontation between paramilitaries, guerrillas and military forces. I was a privileged witness to what happened on the battlefield. I knew the color, smell and sadism of the war. And I decided to keep what happened to me in a drawer, though it was always there, marking and changing my life without mercy.

It was not until 2009, nine years after my kidnapping, that I recognized the necessity of speaking about it, and came to understand that I was among millions of victims of the war in Colombia. It was the result of being asked by the British nongovernmental organization OXFAM to be the voice of a report[2] on sexual violence in Colombia.

The process was not easy, and for the next three years, the decision to talk led me to a deep depression that made me think again about suicide. My sense of "me" crumbled again.

Today, I do not know if that's the price of survival, of having a second chance in life. But I decided to accept it, and a mission emerged from the responsibility to keep on living. And I realized that my voice was not alone anymore. It had become a public outcry, and then a movement, which I named "No es Hora de Callar" ("It's not time to be silent"). This campaign—my campaign—made me an activist, and led me to mix journalism with the defense of human rights.

It has been a long journey since that day in May of 2000, and it has taken me to many places in the world where I could see myself in the eyes of other survivors of sexual violence. Our bodies and our lives are marked by the brutality we experienced, and our task is to prevent other women from having to face the same thing.

My life is still threatened, my case goes unpunished, and I do not know when those who hurt me 15 years ago will be brought to justice, if ever. But I know that even if I cease to exist, and my work is shut down, it will continue in the voices and lives of thousands of women like me.

My struggle led the president of Colombia, Juan Manuel Santos, to declare May 25— the date of my abduction—National Day for the Dignity of Women Victims of Sexual Violence. That is an acknowledgment. But it is important to take action. Our words, our will, can prevent the silencing of voices, the violation of our freedom of expression, and the violation of women through sexual violence.

The deepest pain led me to understand that my strength was in words. My words saved me because they gave meaning to my life. To those who read this today, I want to say that their words can transform the lives of others. Words can indeed change the world. And we, as journalists, have a huge responsibility in this regard. Our words can stir a fight or bury the hope of change forever.

■ ■ ■

Jineth Bedoya Lima is deputy editor of the Colombian newspaper El Tiempo.

2. My Islamic State Social Network

By *Alessandria Masi*

A member of Islamic State sent the author a message, which translates as: "When you have understood the value of this box once it is sealed, you will have understood a reason for this garment."

Source: Alessandria Masi

My first conversation with Islamic State was about my reporting. I had just shared an article I'd written about the terrorist group recruiting Western fighters on my Twitter when I saw that someone using the Twitter handle Abu Omar had also posted a link to the piece on his own account. His profile photo unabashedly displayed the black and white IS flag. As I clicked around his profile, I received a Twitter message from him:

"Your article is pretty good," he wrote in English. "But it lacks some important details." Abu Omar is not his real name; it's his preferred nom de guerre. I've agreed to use pseudonyms for all my Islamic State contacts because they do not want their identities known, and it's important for me to have access to them.

I thanked him for his feedback, careful to craft a response that wouldn't scare him off. A few messages later, he was ranting about atrocities committed by the West and how IS is defending Muslims. Abu Omar said he was in Syria with Islamic State. I was continents away, in my apartment in Brooklyn. We exchanged Twitter messages until 4 a.m.

I got Abu Omar's first message in September 2014, two months after the group bulldozed the border between Syria and Iraq and declared itself an "Islamic State." The IS frenzy had just begun in Western media and, at this point, most people knew only two things about the group: It was one of the most brutal we'd ever seen and had a team of social media masterminds. These are two of their most important recruitment tactics, both of which I had noted in my article, which was published in *International Business Times*.

The Vietnam War brought conflict reporting to television sets in American living rooms, shocking the American public with the horrors of combat and undermining support for military action. During the Iraq War, the U.S. government made sure to curb this press free-for-all and sought to control content by offering journalists a chance to embed with army units and attend daily press briefings. The war in Syria began yet another new chapter of war reporting, bringing the conflict in real time to anyone with a social media account. Many journalists, including me, were thrown into new territory when it came to vetting sources we spoke with on social media. There were no rules and, in many cases, there were no methods for being 100 percent sure that what you were seeing on YouTube or Facebook was true.

In the early stages, the only way to learn about Islamic State was to click through the hundreds of photo reports, videos, monthly military roundups and magazines the group published online. They did not talk to press. If you wanted a comment from the group's leader, Abu Bakr al-Baghdadi, you had to wait until he released a statement. By late 2015, there had been only five.

Since my first conversation with Abu Omar, I've come up with my own makeshift vetting system for online reporting. Generally, I speak to rebels, activists, militants or even civilians in the region nearly every day for a month before treating them as a credible source. We chat about the current situation in their location and, more importantly, their opinions. A pro-regime fighter will have a very different outlook than a Syrian rebel and it's imperative to know which side they're coming from before publishing what they have to say.

During that first month, both their answers to my questions and their communication style (the time of day and amount of time they're able to chat) contribute to the vetting process. If they have an unreliable Internet connection, or tell me that they can speak only in certain areas (in the hospital, for example), they are much more likely to be telling the truth than someone who claims to be texting from the frontlines. If they pass the first month, I will then try to set up a video conversation or phone call to confirm their whereabouts.

Unlike many of my colleagues, I never quote Islamic State fighters in articles mainly because their true identity is too difficult to confirm. My conversations with IS fighters serve only to help me understand the group better when conducting my own reporting. To publish what they said would just turn me into one of their propaganda mechanisms. For this piece, I have chosen to publish snippets of my conversations because they illuminate the group's online supporters' views of women, which makes their physical location much less vital.

But because Abu Omar was my first IS contact, I hadn't developed this system yet. I wasn't sure how to confirm his identity and make sure he wasn't just an Islamic State fanboy in his mother's basement in New Jersey posing as the real thing (not that this type of source isn't without its benefits when trying to learn about the group).

I knew I couldn't use it in my reporting, but that didn't stop me from trying to learn about Islamic State from Abu Omar. I told him that my article, like many other accounts in the Western media, lacked important information because I was a female journalist and his "brothers" in IS wouldn't speak to me. Perhaps he could help me.

"You are very clever," he wrote. "There is a reason why we do not speak to the media."

Online reporters generally make their own set of rules for self-preservation. Don't read the comments. Don't engage the trolls on Twitter. Don't answer demeaning Facebook messages. Don't respond to hate emails. Being a woman reporter online involves following the same rules, but the insults generally stem from my gender and not my work.

I have been hacked by the Syrian Electronic Army for writing an article that was critical of Syrian president Bashar Assad and asked how many people I have to have sexual relations with to get my article published. Hackers affiliated with the Syrian regime accessed the *International Business Times* website, removed my article, and replaced it with a threat to remove all of our content if I ever wrote about Syria again. An hour later, I republished the article.

One particularly angry Twitter user publicly posted that I should try to work at *Elle* or *Vogue* magazine and "stick to what you know." I have been accused of being a traitor, liar, prostitute, terrorist, Zionist, crusader and—my personal favorite—a fake Canadian. Notably, my IS contacts were careful not to isolate my work due to my gender, presumably because doing so would undermine their agenda, but that agenda was apparent in other, sometimes subtle, ways. I assume they didn't isolate my work by gender because they didn't care about my work, only that I was a woman.

Mainly, Abu Omar complained that as a journalist, I was part of this Western media conspiracy that was propagating lies about IS brutality. I was ready for him to start verbally assaulting me, but it never happened—not even when I provoked him by asking pointed questions about the so-called Islamic State.

At around 2 a.m., I grew tired of hearing the same angry complaints about my profession and the United States, the country in which I lived and, until I moved to Beirut, worked. I asked Abu Omar why, if he believed all the vitriol he was condensing into 140-character Twitter messages, he was risking having a conversation with me.

"Allah has put us on the same path so that I may help you see light and understand the truth," he wrote.

Among the challenges and potential benefits of engaging Islamic State in such conversations as a single, female, non–Muslim journalist was that they were intent on manipulating me, using my gender to recruit me to their cause. For the most part, they perceived me as weak and tried to shelter me from the horrors happening on the ground. But on the other hand, not viewing me as a threat made them feel comfortable enough to speak honestly about other topics, such as daily life in the so-called caliphate and their views on women. In my conversations with Abu Omar and others, it was clear that they believed my mind could still be changed from afar. I had to be taught the proper way for a good woman to live and then I would believe what they told me: Islamic State was actually protecting and defending the rights of respectable Muslim women.

Abu Omar's feedback on my article had been spot on. I had missed one key point that is central to IS's recruitment strategy: courting women into the caliphate. Dozens of women were going to Syria to join the group, nearly all of them having been courted, charmed and often converted through encounters with their own Abu Omars.

My gender makes it impossible for IS fighters online to think of me as anything other than a woman—least of all a journalist. Working in a profession that is dominated by men, I would never tolerate this sort of behavior from another male source or male colleagues, but because I knew that Abu Omar was trying to recruit me, I had two options: I could end my conversation with him and miss the opportunity to learn about Islamic State's female recruitment process and, possibly, how they justify their brutal behavior; or I could grin and bear the blatantly sexist treatment, pretending I didn't know what he was trying to do, in hopes that I could tap information that would not be available to me if I were a male reporter.

I chose the latter, and in so doing, found myself reporting on Islamic State as if through some surreptitious online dating site.

■ ■ ■

Several factors contributed to my decision to go with option two, but the tipping point began when Mosul, Iraq, fell in June 2014. I was a breaking news reporter at *International Business Times*, working the night shift and splitting my coverage between brief snippets of the Gaza War, the rise of IS and the launch of Game of Thrones-themed beer, hoping that one day I'd get the opportunity to be the Middle East reporter.

I was just two months into the job and, because I was mostly working nights, I didn't have much direct contact with the senior editors. Then, one afternoon, I began to see photos of a familiar face appear in nearly every tweet in my IS Twitter list. The thumbnail-sized photos weren't clear, but I could just make out that the person was wearing orange. I wasn't sure what had happened, but I knew that everyone on this list was tweeting the same thing; it meant they were happy about something and that was bad news for us. I jumped up from my gray cubicle and yelled to no one in particular: "I think something bad just happened."

Seconds after my outburst, the editor-in-chief, breaking news editor, Middle East reporter and international editor stood behind me as I sat at my computer, all of us watching as the IS militant soon-to-be-known-as Jihadi John issued threats to President Obama with a knife in one hand and a fistful of captive journalist James Foley's orange jumpsuit in the other. Foley, as all the world now knows, was then beheaded.

I went home angry that night. I called my father, my friends, my grandparents and anyone else who would answer, so that I could tell them what happened. The Islamic State group had just changed the nature of reporting on the conflict. They had just killed a man for doing his job, for doing all of our jobs. We weren't just observers anymore. Though reporters had been targeted before, including Daniel Pearl, IS was now institutionalizing our systematic murder. Our vests emblazoned with the word PRESS were now a risk, not a safety measure.

It seems a little strange to me now, but none of my editors questioned the validity of my sources for that first IS video. A few weeks later, when Abu Omar sent me the first Islamic State propaganda video of British journalist and IS captive John Cantlie, one editor actually commended me for receiving it before most other news outlets.

I had just become the newsroom's unofficial IS reporter, which meant having to watch nearly all of the group's gruesome videos after that first one. It may sound perverse, but I couldn't stop watching. I became obsessed with what seemed like a personal betrayal. I felt like they had taken away my dream: I couldn't be the reporter I had wanted to be because, despite the calm conservations I had engaged in with Abu Omar and others, they had made it acceptable to execute me for doing my work. And my way of dealing with that was to try to understand why.

■ ■ ■

During the next year and a half, a handful of IS fighters inadvertently taught me about their ideology by trying to justify the hundreds of photos and videos of Islamic State crucifixions, beheadings, drownings, mass executions, rapes and sex slaves I had seen. During those conversations, my gender came into play in two ways: They spoke to me because they were trying to recruit me, as a woman, to Syria; and they were careful not to send me offensive or harsh propaganda. Most journalists receive gruesome photos and bloody videos from fighters and activists alike, but I have never received anything worse than a selfie from IS fighters. Any brutal propaganda I watched came from what I was able to find online through my own research.

The conversations always start with the same small talk and questions that form the basis of any first meeting. But almost immediately after, the IS fighter makes his goal clear by asking two telltale questions.

Are you a Muslim? No.

Are you married? No.

They then try to convince me to join them in Syria, even though every self-proclaimed IS fighter with whom I've spoken knows I'm a journalist. I use my official social media accounts and the same picture I have on the *International Business Times* website.

I tried to defend my profession and demanded to know why Islamic State had made it a habit to execute journalists. Most of the IS members answered with some excuse that had already been disseminated in the group's online propaganda. The journalists were spies, they were CIA, they were members of the Israeli Mossad, and they were tools of the White House. They never said they killed them just for being journalists, and they assured me that as long as I was honest in my reporting about the IS agenda, I would not be harmed.

Their answers did not surprise me, as most of the IS fighters with whom I spoke were much more eager to begin with recruitment than to discuss being a journalist.

Abu Abdullah, a former architect in Algeria, was fighting with IS in Iraq during the summer of 2015 when he reached out to me on Twitter. Muslim? No. Married? No.

"Now I looking for woman," he wrote.

"I can't find a girl."

"Do you understand me?"

He didn't have much time to recruit me. It was already June, Ramadan was about to begin, and he hoped to be married by Eid al-Fitr, the celebration at the close of the holy month.

I asked Abdullah why he was looking for a woman when I had been told that IS provided brides for its fighters. I was wrong, he said. Finding a bride involved telling the imam that you had found your future wife and asking her father for his permission. Once her father has agreed, "the girl must see the boy and then she decides."

Abu Abdullah had in fact joined IS to protect good Muslim women, he claimed. In other religions, he said, women are treated "like a product."

"I can't see Muslim girls be violated by anyone anymore. Our women and girls are our honor, understand this."

There were families in Iraq from Canada and the U.S., he told me, and he sent me photos of his friends' children, draped in IS paraphernalia and holding assault rifles as tall as they were. He also sent me photos of him in his former job as an architect and selfies of him on Iraq's battlefields. We talked about his favorite architectural structures and he told me how great his life was now that he was in the caliphate.

He added me on WhatsApp a few days later and immediately asked me to remove my profile picture because my hair was uncovered. The first time we Skyped, so that he could show me how "great" life was in Mosul, Iraq, he initially hung up on me because my hair "shocked him." He called back, but I did not cover my hair.

For weeks after that, he sent me e-books about Islam and sermons from prominent religious leaders, even though I told him I am Catholic. He explained the benefits and importance of wearing a hijab and sent me reading material to back up his statements. If I didn't respond he would continue to send the messages until I did.

I told Abu Abdullah that from what I knew about the treatment of women in the caliphate, it was not as good as he made it sound. In the official list of IS fatwas (Islamic rulings), women are prevented from being alone with men or shaking their hands, showing their eyes or any part of their face, or wearing perfume, among many other rules. (Oddly enough, bleaching one's eyebrows is permissible, according to the fatwas.)

But what actually happened on the ground was much more gruesome than what the fatwas suggested. Human Rights Watch documented a "system of organized rape and sexual assault, sexual slavery, and forced marriage by ISIS forces" against Yazidi women that they had taken hostage during their attack on Mount Sinjar, Iraq. In fact, I had written an article about a video that showed IS fighters discussing their upcoming visit to a slave market of Yazidi women. The men in the video spoke with grotesque excitement as they bantered about payment and tried to buy each other's share of slave women.

"The price differs if she has blue eyes," said a fighter who had chin-length dark hair and a gold ring on his pinky finger and who was addressed as Abu Fahd in the video. "If she is 15 years old ... I have to check her teeth." The other fighters all laughed.

"If she doesn't have teeth, why would I want her?" Abu Fahd asked in an incredulous tone.

It repulsed me, but I never asked Abdullah about this video because I knew his response would be the same as Abu Omar's response the year before: These claims were just propaganda.

Perhaps I was being naive, but I believed that Abdullah sincerely thought he was defending women's rights, though I knew it was limited to Muslim women. So when I heard the Turkish government accuse a female IS suicide bomber of carrying out the devastating attack in the Turkish town of Suruc on the border with Syria in the summer of 2015, I asked Abdullah how he could have let this happen to a woman. Abdullah sounded as surprised as I was to hear the news.

"I have no information I will check," he wrote.

Two days later, I got a simple answer: "It wasn't us. The Caliph refuses to use women or to let them carry out suicide attacks."

He wasn't lying. Women are an essential part of Islamic State's infrastructure, but do not typically have a combat role. Instead, female recruits are responsible for running schools in IS territory, keeping the rest of the women in line, and acting as online recruiters for other foreign women. Of all the suicide attacks IS has carried out around the region, I know of none in which they used a female bomber. (The Turkish government later announced that the bomber was not a woman.) Though IS has banned women from fighting on the frontlines, the group has published a document stating exceptions for women who want to participate. A woman is allowed to wear and detonate an explosive device without permission if she is in Saudi Arabia; if she is being "raided" in her home and no one else is around; or if the emir has permitted it or if it is for the public good.

Abu Abdullah messaged me nearly every day until September, including on Eid, when Ramadan ended. I don't think he ever got married.

I vetted Abdullah using my own process, like all the others, and his answers were by far the most believable. His interest in me had nothing to do with my reporting; in fact, the only time we discussed my profession was when he needed help making a different Facebook account (I worked at a website so I must know how to help him, he said). I can't explain why, but he never worried that I would publish any of the videos or information he sent me.

Although most IS contacts assumed my gender rendered me harmless, some were not as trusting as Abu Abdullah and Abu Omar. Abu Ahmad, a young Tunisian fighter in Raqqa, was the most skeptical of me. He had reason to believe he was being monitored: His Twitter account had been twice suspended during the time we spoke to each other, probably because his cover image was a group photo of IS fighters smiling for the camera. When he initially contacted me on Twitter, he mistakenly thought that I was a French man.

"Brother, do you want to come to sham?" he asked, using the ancient word for Greater Syria borrowed from the Umayyad Dynasty. "I get requests to come from French people every day."

After he realized who I was, and what I do for a living, I told him I knew of an upcoming attack that IS had planned in Berlin. One of my non-IS sources in Tunisia had tipped me off to the attack a week before while I was in Paris covering the gruesome attacks at the French satirical newspaper *Charlie Hebdo*. The Tunisian source was still in my one-month vetting process, so I did not publish anything about his claim, but by asking Ahmad about it, I was trying to confirm both his and the Tunisian's information.

Ahmad immediately became paranoid. He was adamant about finding out who had told me about the attack. He was nervous that someone in Raqqa would accuse him of giving journalists information. A few days after our initial exchange, I received another message from him:

"You have troubled me since you wrote that you knew of an attack. What do you know about it exactly? How did your source find out, and if he was really in the know, why would he speak about it with you?"

For the Tunisian source's protection, I never divulged his identity to Ahmad. I told Ahmad that he was under no obligation to speak to me if he was uncomfortable. Less than a week later, German police arrested three men for recruiting and providing financial support to Islamic State, thwarting a potential attack. Even after the arrest, Ahmad continued asking for a few weeks until, finally, he disappeared.

■ ■ ■

All of the IS members I've spoken with eventually give up on recruiting me, become paranoid because I'm a journalist, and disappear, deleting their social media accounts and changing their WhatsApp or Viber phone numbers. Some of them have probably been killed, but most fighters have ended our conversations because they were afraid of getting caught.

Two weeks of back-and-forth messaging after our first conversation in September 2014, Abu Omar disappeared from my Twitter. A few hours later he made a Facebook page and I was his only friend. He wrote to me immediately and deleted the account once I had received the message.

"It's me Abu Omar. I can't speak to you anymore. We are living in a digital cage," he wrote. "Insha'allah [God willing] we shall meet when the Khalifa expands."

Abu Omar is not the only one that IS has placed in a digital cage. They have done the same to journalists. The only way reporters writing about Islamic State can do their jobs safely is to remain in the cage the group has created, protected by distance and anonymity, courtesy of the Internet.

This story would have a much different ending had I ever met any of these men in real life. Speaking to them online put enough distance between us that I could try to ignore their blatant objectification of women. Had we ever met in person, I'm not sure I would have been able to hide the disgust I felt, and that would have probably landed me in the same position as the Yazidi women.

In my conversations with Islamic State members I often had to ignore my instinct to demand that women be treated equally. I'm not proud of suppressing that instinct, but it's something I felt was necessary to better understand the role of women within the group. I had to become one of the women the group would target for recruitment in order to learn about it. In a way, it's like a new form of embedded journalism, one that can exist only online—and for a woman.

■ ■ ■

Alessandria Masi is the Middle East correspondent focused on all things terrorism for International Business Times. *She is a native of Montreal and is based in Beirut.*

3. Why a Troll Trolls

By Elisabeth Witchel

Afghan women at an Internet café in Kabul. Online trolling has become a major concern for activists and journalists, particularly females.

Source: Reuters/Mohammad Ismail

"Yeah ... I went too far," he said, which by most accounts would be an understatement.

Among the Twitter comments this Internet troll posted to or about a female writer and activist were:

"Rape her nice ass."

"I will find you."

"The police will do nothing."

The man, who agreed to be interviewed only under a pseudonym—we'll call him Jim—said he did not start off with the intention of menacing anyone. Yet it is hard to imagine a public milieu where an individual might consider casually uttering such words—to a stranger no less.

Jim's comments are, however, disturbingly representative of Internet trolling, a practice that has become a major concern for activists and journalists, particularly females.

A troll, or more specifically a cyber troll, is commonly described as a person who intentionally posts provocative messages to cause arguments or disruptions. The term has come to be applied broadly to a range of online behaviors, from those that are provocatively contrarian to others that are criminally menacing. Trolls may target specific individuals and they may stand out in a virtual crowd or operate like a mob, tearing apart anyone whose views, appearance or attitude they don't like.

Online hectoring directly affects nearly half the cyber community, according to a 2014 study[1] by the U.S.-based Pew Research Center, which found that 40 percent of Internet users have personally experienced mild to severe online harassment. Men are more often subject to insults online, according to the study, but forms of online abuse toward women tend to be far more severe, including sexual harassment and threats of violence. "The kinds of threats women get online are in sync with the real-world threats they face," said feminist activist and writer Soraya Chemaly.

This special brand of online abuse is becoming a de facto occupational hazard for many female journalists. Sri Lankan journalist Sonali Samarasinghe describes the negative comments she has received online as typically criticizing not her words but her womanhood. "One person wrote that I had no uterus," she recalled.

Samarasinghe is not alone. A March 2014 survey[2] on violence and harassment against women in media conducted by the International News Safety Institute and the International Women's Media Foundation found that a quarter of the work-related threats and intimidation directed at female journalists took place online.

Though the impact and prevalence of Internet abuse and trolling are increasingly well documented and aired in public forums, less is known about those who engage in it and why. The anonymity and fluidity of social media, and the fact that trolls come in many shapes and sizes, make it hard to pin down an archetype. "It's really important to remember that underneath all their abuse, trolls are complex human beings just like the rest of us," noted Claire Hardaker, a linguist at Lancaster University who has written extensively on trolls. "They can be women in their twenties, men in their twenties, or thirties, or sixties— mothers, fathers, privately educated, or from any walk of life at all."

Despite their penchant for inserting themselves into online threads, contacting trolls directly for this report proved challenging. Many accounts had been shut down or banned and several trolls did not respond to or refused interview requests.

In a phone interview, Jim said that he began tweeting comments when he was a newcomer to social media, exploring topics that were trending on Twitter. "I decided for some stupid reason to join in," he said. Once the retweets and responses began flowing, he felt a strong personal validation and so embarked upon what soon became an ugly trajectory. His explanation of how that happened doesn't fully account for the brutishness that resulted, but it does provide insight into the pull of trolling.

Another troll—though he does not approve of that appellation— who identifies himself on Twitter as @SageCommander, also known as John Blackout, calls himself an "irritant," not a troll. "I like to 'troll' certain accounts, especially when they tweet something stupid," he said in an interview via Twitter. "But I don't consider myself a troll. My tweets are maybe 20 percent trolling."

Blackout sees his online comments not as harassment but as a needed counterweight to opinions and news items he believes are flawed. "I can make people uncomfortable when confronting them with their own positions," he wrote. For him, it is dialectic without boundaries. "I might ask someone who considers themselves 'pro-choice' if they are ok with aborting babies at nine months so long as at least part of them is still in the mother. That isn't trolling—it's asking them to examine the courage and extremes of their position."

For some, such comments border on, or cross over into, hate speech. While women are often victims of online aggression, some of the worst trolling targets race.

Andrew Auernheimer, as he identifies himself, also known as @rabide, and sometimes as weev, revels in the opportunity provided by social media and the blogosphere to tout his Aryan causes, among them #WhiteGenocide. "I've never harassed anyone in legal definitions, but some people see Aryan opinions as harassment," he said in a phone interview. Though Auernheimer now focuses on nationalist and racist complaints, he said his interest in trolling escalated with the emergence in 2014 of #gamergate, an online campaign against several women in the gaming industry that spun into a rash of serious cyber harassment, including threats[3] of violence and doxxing, the practice of revealing personal information, such as home addresses, online.

Auernheimer was imprisoned for more than three years for hacking and identity fraud. On his account he has posted, "The thing I missed most in prison was Twitter. Seriously." He said Twitter gives him an entrée he never had into the pop culture fray. Prior to Twitter, "there was not a single outlet to represent us; we were shunned by the mainstream." He has more than 29,000 followers.

Auernheimer explained trolling as a weapon in his war against "SJWs," or social justice warriors. One of its most powerful functions, he said, is to push the "Overton window"—a political theory[4] developed by American public policy analyst Joseph Overton to describe the range of ideas the public will accept. Auernheimer claims the numbers of like-minded "netizens" are growing. "It's a great time to be a white nationalist!" he said.

Some efforts have been made in recent years to identify the social and psychological causes behind trolling. According to one study,[5] "Trolls Just Want to Have Fun," which looks into the personality traits of trolls, they are simply bad people. The study, published in 2014 by Canadian psychology academics Erin E. Buckels, Paul D. Trapnell and

Delroy L. Paulhus, found "trolling correlated positively with sadism, psychopathy, and Machiavellianism," with sadism showing the most "robust" associations with trolling. "Cyber-trolling appears to be an Internet manifestation of everyday sadism," the authors concluded.

But there is a danger, others contend, in marginalizing trolls as malevolent outliers or social aberrations. "It lends itself to a mythology, but in fact they are 'normal,' reflecting a dimension of human nature that is ugly," said Chemaly, who writes on gender for *The Huffington Post*, the *Guardian* and other publications. Trolls frequently target women and "The word itself evokes some little monster, but we are talking about the misogynists next door," she said.

Trolling has become so pervasive that one U.K. insurance company offers policies[6] that include coverage of the costs of legal action, relocation and other actions necessitated by cyberbullying.

Whitney Phillips, author of the book *This Is Why We Can't Have Nice Things: Mapping the Relationship Between Online Trolling and Mainstream Culture*,[7] argues that trolling is a manifestation of deeper societal problems, such as pervasive sexism. "This isn't a 'trolling' issue, in other words, it's evidence of a cultural sickness," Phillips said in an email. "I would argue that more commonplace, everyday expressions of sexism are just as dangerous as more extreme, obvious examples of violent misogyny."

Hardaker, the Lancaster University linguistics lecturer, agrees, though for different reasons, that viewing trolls through a more universal lens is the best approach to understanding their behavior. "Very few of us look at ourselves in the mirror that morning and say, 'Today I'm going to attack a child online till they cry, self-harm, or even commit suicide,'" she said. "Instead, they're likely to be thinking of their behavior in other, more socially acceptable ways—they're correcting people who are wrong, they're sticking it to the man, they're righting a perceived wrong, they're just being funny for their friends, and so forth."

How, then, to deal with the problem of trolls, which sometimes threatens to escalate into actual violence? And at what point do gender-based trolling attacks actually encourage the kind of pervasive sexism Phillips evoked?

A handful of women have confronted their cyber persecutors successfully, either directly or through legal action. In 2014, Seattle-based writer and editor Lindy West wrote an open letter online to one of her trolls. Her antagonist had made derogatory comments while impersonating West's recently deceased father. Surprisingly, the troll apologized via email. West chronicled the exchange for National Public Radio's *This American Life* program,[8] during which the two also spoke by phone. He explained that his actions stemmed from his offense at seeing a highly confident woman at a time when he was professionally frustrated and had recently broken up with a girlfriend.

"I think my anger towards you stems from your happiness with your own being," he wrote in an email to West. "It offended me because it served to highlight my unhappiness with my own self. It is the lowest thing I have ever done."

Women's activist and writer Caroline Criado-Perez, whose campaign[9] to put Jane Austen on Great Britain's 10-pound note brought her a maelstrom of online rape and death threats, brought charges against two of her worst trollers, including a woman, Isabella Sorley. Both were jailed[10] in January 2014 for making "extreme threats." In a public apology on BBC, Sorley read some of her tweets aloud.[11] They included "Rape is the last of your worries" and "Go kill yourself before I do." She described her behavior as "utterly appalling." "It's disgusting, it's venomous," she said, and though she attributed it to alcohol, she admitted there must be more to it. "Am I mental? I've got to question," she said in the interview.

The conventional wisdom, however, is that "feeding the troll" by responding or confronting him typically leads to more aggressive activities, rather than trolls' remorse. Jim said he escalated the vehemence of his comments the moment his target began to snipe back, though he did not say why.

"They want attention. If you respond, they win" is how University of Pennsylvania professor Anthea Butler sees it. Butler said she has had to block thousands of accounts due to hostile comments.

Those who troll often say that anyone unhappy with what is being said can simply leave the conservation. John Blackout said that in his opinion it is up to the individual user to draw the line of what he or she will tolerate. "Other people can decide whether to follow/fave/retweet/mute/block and control their own timeline," he said.

For journalists, that is easier said than done, according to U.S. journalist and founder of TrollBusters Michele Ferrier, who chronicles her own experience with hateful readers elsewhere in this book. "If your job is being public as a journalist, you cannot avoid social media as part of your job," she said. "It's expected to be online in many capacities. Or if you are an independent online news provider, who are you going to call to step in for you?" Ignoring physical threats can be risky, she said. "There is no safe space online and limited recourse to just block or get off the computer."

So the trolling continues. Jim said he plans to stop trolling, but whether he will manage to overcome the urge remains to be seen.

■ ■ ■

Elisabeth Witchel, a CPJ consultant, previously worked as the organization's journalist assistance coordinator. She also launched CPJ's Global Campaign Against Impunity.

4. Preparing for the Worst

By Karen Coates

Cassandra Giraldo, a reporting fellow with the International Women's Media Foundation, participates in a hostage scenario during security training in Uganda.

Source: Katie Moore

I t's a calm day in a Ugandan village. Women gather on plastic chairs, shaded from the afternoon sun. I'm here with a handful of journalists on a reporting trip sponsored by the International Women's Media Foundation (IWMF). The village women welcome us and begin to tell us about their lives. Then something happens. A man in the shadows glares at us. Others begin to crowd around. There is tension. We are not wanted here.

They come from all directions, waving canes and bamboo poles. We run. They chase. We sprint around a building, toward the far side of the village, as the mob closes in. There's a wall, and we can't jump it. We have no choice but to turn and face the gang.

My heart pounds: It's us—with notebooks, cameras and recorders— against a dozen villagers with sticks. I grab my colleague's hand and we brace our bodies for impact, barging through the horde and running toward our car. All of us make it out unharmed but rattled.

This is all a test, part of hostile environments training for female journalists, conducted by Global Journalist Security (GJS). The anger isn't real, and neither is the mob. But almost everything else is—the Ugandan sunshine, the IWMF reporters, the women, the sticks, the wall and the pounding in my heart. It's all meant to be an exercise in dealing with sudden dangers and unexpected attacks, in this case with the specter of villagers in a conflict-ridden society who are suspicious of our activities as journalists. Though the mob and village women are actors hired by GJS, and the reporters hail from multiple countries, with the largest contingent from the United States, when I see that wall and turn to face the mob I have unexpected flashbacks of riots I've covered in Southeast Asia. As a journalist, I've faced gunfire, robberies, a grenade attack, government surveillance, detainment and deportation. But until now I had never been trained to cope with any of that.

■ ■ ■

At the time we underwent our training, nine months into 2015, the year already ranked among the deadliest on record for working journalists. By the end of the year, at least 71 journalists were killed in direct relation to their work, according to CPJ research.[1] In more than two-thirds of those cases, the journalist was singled out for murder.[2]

"Journalists today face more threats to their physical safety because they have become targets," said Lily Hindy, deputy director of Reporters Instructed in Saving Colleagues (RISC). "Before they were in danger simply because they were close to it and could be caught in the crossfire; now they are sought out specifically."

Female journalists face certain dangers, such as sexual assault and sexual harassment, far more often than men, which is why gender-specific security training, such as the IWMF hosts, is becoming more widespread and increasingly viewed as essential.

In 2014, IWMF and the International News Safety Institute (INSI) published "Violence and Harassment Against Women in the News Media,"[3] billed as the first comprehensive report on threats to female journalists around the globe. "Nearly two-thirds of survey respondents said they had experienced some form of intimidation, threats, or abuse in relation to their work, ranging in severity from name-calling to death threats," IWMF Executive Director Elisa Lees Muñoz told me in an email interview. Most of those incidents were never reported, and most "occurred in the workplace rather than on assignment." Still, many women reported incidents of physical violence—pushing, shoving, assault with an object or weapon—that happened in the field while covering protests, rallies or public events. More than 14 percent of respondents said they'd experienced sexual violence related to their jobs; nearly half of all respondents said they'd endured sexual harassment.

"Women are at greater risk of being sexually assaulted than men, both by individual and group male attackers, as well as by sexually aggressive mobs," said Frank Smyth, GJS executive director and CPJ's senior adviser for journalist security. It is unclear whether those risks have increased, he said, "or if women and men among the press corps have recently brought more attention to the issue by finally talking about it."

The issue gained global attention in 2011 when a mob sexually assaulted CBS News correspondent and CPJ board member Lara Logan, who was covering the uprisings in Egypt's Tahrir Square, a notoriously dangerous place for reporters.[4] British journalist Natasha Smith recounted a similar incident.[5] And in 2013, a Dutch journalist was raped while covering protests in the same location.[6] They aren't alone: Photojournalist Lynsey Addario described her kidnapping and assault[7] in Libya in gripping detail in her memoir, *It's What I Do*.[8]

Many journalists have said enough is enough. And they're acting.

"We made the decision that wherever possible we would offer hostile environments training to any women with whom we work," IWMF's Muñoz said. "We believe that it is our responsibility."

That includes the GJS training that puts me in a make-believe mob in Uganda. It is one of several role-play scenarios—kidnapping, car wreck, shootings, grenades, sniper attacks—we work through individually and as a group.

■ ■ ■

"We will push you out of your comfort zone," Smyth tells us on Day 1 of our training. But, he adds, "we do not want to traumatize you." Unlike life, I can stop any activity, anytime, by simply raising a hand.

Our three-day course covers everything from emergency first aid to weapons to digital security. I will always remember "DR. ABC": Danger, Response, Airway, Breathing, Circulation. If a colleague is shot in front of me, or a stranger is bleeding from a traffic accident injury, I now know the initial steps for administering emergency aid before seeking help.

As a reporter, I developed early on an instinct for situational awareness—assessing the scene around me, from a broad to a narrow perspective. But I admit I've been lax about formalities: a risk assessment to be conducted before a reporting trip, a communication plan to develop with friends or relatives before departure, and a proof-of-life document that contains confidential information that can be used in worst-case scenarios to confirm whether a person is still alive. (Examples of these forms and a full scope of journalist safety information can be found online through CPJ's Journalist Security Guide[9] and the Rory Peck Trust.[10])

"Look at the worst-case scenario and then prepare for it," said Judith Matloff, a longtime foreign correspondent who offers journalist safety training independently and through Columbia University. "I started covering stuff in the 80s," she said. "Journalists were targeted then. And the risks were immense, but there's an awareness now. We didn't have advocacy groups, we didn't have training groups, we didn't have anything. Our editors would give us like a bottle of scotch and say good luck."

There are far more resources today, but they could be better, Matloff said.

"Very few people actually offer training for women, and it's something that I think has been ignored for too long," Matloff said. Many hostile environments courses are run by men with military training "and what they do is they throw a sack over somebody's head … and say this is what it's like to be kidnapped," she said. "It doesn't prepare you for good decision-making. What it does is it teaches you what it's like when the s*&t hits the fan." Her training focuses instead on how to avoid those situations in the first place.

Though training is key, it is also important to carefully vet the training program itself, Matloff said. In some cases male trainers have too closely mirrored the perpetrators women need to avoid, she said. "I've spoken to countless women who've been hit upon or sexually harassed by the male trainers," she said. "Military men tend to foster a very gung-ho boys'-own type of environment that women don't feel that easy with, so already you're starting out in a situation where women are outside their comfort zone."

Smyth agreed that security trainings designed by the "Western military mindset" aren't the best fit for most reporters in the field. "Journalists and NGO workers are unarmed civilians who are constantly navigating among authorities or others with guns. This requires a broader and more nuanced skillset than traditional military training would provide," he said. Global Journalist Security treats sexual assault sensitively, but openly. Men and women are included in GJS trainings because "both women and men must be part of the solution," he said. "There has long been a taboo about the subject of sexual assault, and whispering about it in small groups only feeds the stigma surrounding it."

Indeed, Matloff said, that stigma prevents many women from talking about an assault after it happens. "There's also the shame that somehow you are a bad professional," she said. "These women feel really, really isolated." And they often don't tell their bosses, "particularly freelancers—they're afraid they're not going to get sent on assignments."

The IWMF/INSI survey confirmed this. "I never reported it. To whom should I report? The same person who intimidated me is the same person to whom under normal circumstances, I was to report," one Cameroonian journalist commented (the survey did not include respondent names).

Another, an American, wrote that she suffered the consequences of reporting on-the-job harassment to her supervisors. "I was the one sent home and removed from my normal responsibilities. Quickly the investigation turned on me."

Many respondents said they suffered both physical and psychological pain from work-related assaults. Some started using a pen name. Others dropped particular stories. Some permanently moved or gave up journalism entirely. As a result, threats against female journalists are often, ultimately, threats against public information.

■ ■ ■

Prevention is key—that's one of the primary lessons in safety training. And often, it comes down to you. "You have no choice but to take care of your own security," Smyth said.

Matloff talks about an experience she had while reporting in Burundi. She'd met a key source, a military official, who wanted to take her out after curfew. "I just knew—I had that uh-oh feeling," she said. She didn't go out with him. "I didn't get the story, I lost him as a source, but I wasn't raped," she said. "We have to make these difficult choices that men don't. A guy could have just gone out drinking with him and it would have been fine." Women must take greater precautions. "Everybody goes down to the bar in the hotel at night," she said. "You've got to be really careful. People slip drugs in your drink, you get drunk … you can't react quickly if you're drunk."

And if something goes wrong, it's critical to have a plan for dealing with worst-case scenarios, Matloff said.

Such questions should also be asked by people with whom the reporters work, she said. "It's a discussion that has to take place in the newsroom before women go out," Matloff said. "The whole industry should be aware of it."

Unfortunately, independent journalists tend to be even more isolated. "Freelance media workers are sometimes at additional risk doing their jobs, as they have none of the institutional resources or support afforded employees of a news organization," according to the IWMF/INSI report.

"Freelance safety is up to both the freelancers themselves and the publishers of their work," said Hindy of RISC. "It is irresponsible for a freelancer to go into a dangerous area without doing a thorough risk assessment, getting prepared through training and carrying the right equipment. It is equally irresponsible for an editor/publisher to pay a freelancer less than they need to safely carry out their assignment, and not ask the right questions about how prepared they are to be doing that assignment. If a freelancer is not trained and a publisher wants to take their work from a conflict zone, we think they should help pay for them to be adequately prepared."

How effective is preparation? "We measure success several ways: by both the direct and anonymous feedback we receive from trainees immediately after classes, by the stories trainees have told about how they have successfully applied the training lessons later in the field, and by our steadily increasing roster of both news and NGO clients," Smyth said.

Freelance reporter Roxanne L. Scott, a 2015 IWMF fellow who participated in security training in Kenya before reporting in the Democratic Republic of the Congo, said her training changed her approach to danger. "Even when I'm not working, I'm always aware of my surroundings," she said. "For example, when I used to get in my car, I'd sit for a while sending text messages, sometimes with the windows opened. The security training taught me there is a risk that someone can walk by and grab my phone out of my hand or try to open my door. So now, when I get in my car, I start it and drive off as soon as I can. I also learned to know who is around you. If I'm in a dark area, I always look around to know who is around so I'm not caught by surprise."

Matloff said she'd like to see hard data on the most useful kinds of security training for female journalists. "I can't give you statistics," she said. "We need to do an industry-wide survey to see what type of training is useful, other than anecdotally." And she believes the survey should come from a neutral, nonprofit source. "It's really hard for a trainer to do that, to allow a really, really thorough analysis of data, of whether what they're doing is effective," she said. "I feel any time that profit gets involved, when you're providing a service, it muddies the situation."

■ ■ ■

That afternoon in Uganda, when the test-mob closes in, I am thinking of protests I have covered in Cambodia. I am thinking of moments I wished I could backpedal through time, to change my steps and avoid the scene entirely.

And yet: That wouldn't work. Even if I could reverse the clock, I'd still probably end up facing the mob—the real mob. As a journalist, it's my chosen job to be where the story is—which is, at times, a risky place. And no training can diminish that impulse in me.

"It's the nature of our profession that we'll never fully be 100 percent safe," said independent journalist Molly McCluskey, a 2014 IWMF fellow who went through security training in Uganda before reporting in the Democratic Republic of the Congo. "Preparation and training help mitigate the risk, but as long as we're in the field, asking questions that people don't want answered, we're going to be in varying levels of danger. To feel more secure, I would have to change professions entirely."

■ ■ ■

A few safety tips for journalists of any gender from security training programs, individual experience and the IWMF/INSI report:

- Conduct a risk assessment before entering a potentially dangerous zone
- Develop a communications plan for checking in with key contacts while in the field
- Prepare a proof-of-life document to be used in case of kidnapping
- Understand the language around you, or hire someone who does
- Stay near the edge of large crowds; avoid the middle

- Always have an escape route
- Research local hospitals before traveling
- Have an evacuation plan
- Know how you will store your information and how you will get it out of the country
- Understand how your work affects the safety of sources, fixers and local journalists

■ ■ ■

Karen Coates *is a senior fellow at Brandeis University's Schuster Institute for Investigative Journalism. She traveled to Uganda and Rwanda on a 2015 International Women's Media Foundation reporting fellowship.*

5. LGBT Reporting in Africa

By Jake Naughton

S., a gay refugee, outside his home in Nairobi. In Kenya, reporting on LGBT issues brings security risks.

Source: Jake Naughton

On a recent trip to Kenya, I sat with S., a gay refugee from the Democratic Republic of Congo, in the cramped, one-room apartment he shares with three friends, all straight. The four share a bed, and none know S. is gay. The floor is covered in a vibrant yellow vinyl, their belongings clutter every corner, and a tiny couch is crammed into the space between the bed and the door.

We were talking about what it's like for him to be a gay refugee in a country that would rather not talk about refugees or gay people. Following the terrorist attack on Westgate Mall in Nairobi that killed more than 60 people and injured 175 others, Kenya began a serious crackdown on foreigners and demanded all refugees go to one of the country's two refugee camps. In part, as a result of the efforts of religious groups both domestic and international, homophobia and anti-gay rhetoric have also been on the rise in recent years, as *Global Post* reported on June 15, 2015.[1] Neither is good for S.'s sense of safety.

S. told me that he had been run out of his previous apartment by his landlord and a band of thugs after they found him and his then-boyfriend together. He showed me the scar where they beat him, and talked about what it's like to share a bed with people who may wish you violence, or even death.

Then his roommates walked through the open door.

I froze and S. immediately switched into a gregarious bravado, joking and laughing with his friends. The entire time we had been talking, I had been eyeing the open door, fearful that we might be overheard, and that the same violence S. was recounting to me would come to pass again. S., too, had been watching, but he took his friends' entry in stride. Constant vigilance was a necessity for him.

So it was for every LGBT refugee I spoke with during two recent trips to Kenya reporting on their experiences. Security is of the utmost concern for them, and nearly every person I spoke with had a story of being attacked by neighbors or random people on the street. Most were living in some degree of hiding and were largely confined to their apartments while they waited out the resettlement process.

I had been connected to the LGBT refugees through another reporter, Jacob Kushner, with whom I was collaborating on a story about their experiences. He, in turn, had been introduced to the refugees by Victor Mukasa, the executive director of the Kuchu Diaspora

Alliance USA, an LGBT diaspora group working with LGBT Africans. Throughout the process, the people we spoke with connected us to others, as is often the case.

Building trust among a group of people who have survived extreme trauma, often at the hands of their closest contacts, is no easy feat, and it is all the more challenging when day-to-day safety remains a serious concern. For LGBT-identifying journalists such as myself, being an LGBT reporter working on LGBT issues can be both a serious boon and a potential risk. I had told S. I was gay almost as soon as we met. As a photographer who frequently works on LGBT stories, I've found being gay and being forthright with my sources about my sexuality go a long way toward making them feel comfortable sharing personal details. And in cases like my reporting outlined earlier, where security is such a fundamental concern, it lends me crucial credibility and the confidence that I won't expose them. (I, too, know the stakes.)

As always, and specifically in instances of trauma, where the authorities are hostile or pose a danger to victims, verification was an issue. Luckily, nearly every refugee I photographed during this project was in the process of having their LGBT refugee status vetted by the United Nations High Commissioner for Refugees (UNHCR), and depending on how far along they were in the resettlement process, by the U.S. or another host country. This vetting typically involves lengthy interviews, pitting the claims of the would-be refugee against hundreds of similar stories told before theirs, as well as comparing their testimony to what is known about the conditions in their specific country for LGBT people. If their claims are deemed credible, they are given U.N. refugee status and moved to the next stage of the process.

Vetting and verifying the specifics of each person's story are difficult but not impossible. Another refugee I met and photographed, Cynthia Ndikumana, is a lesbian refugee from Burundi. She was an LGBT activist in her home country and spoke on BBC radio about being a lesbian there. In 2013 police arrested and beat her, and in late 2014 she fled Burundi in search of safety elsewhere. Because she was out in her home country, she had no problem being photographed and discussing her experiences on the record. Other refugees we met had similar situations. Many of the refugees we spoke with had been outed in the press in their home countries and had photos or videos of the relevant newspapers or television programs. Others had hospital or clinic reports and photos of the aftermath of police or mob violence.

But there were at least as many who preferred we use pseudonyms, nicknames or first initials, as much for the safety of their family members back home as for their own. And many of those stories had details that would be difficult to verify, and potentially put the subject in harm's way. As much as possible, we sought out sources whose stories could be on the record and who had a body of evidence that we could refer to. Luckily, the refugee process generates a fair amount of it.

Recently, I was in Kakuma Refugee Camp in northwest Kenya, alongside the reporter with whom I am working, in the midst of a tense Q-and-A between us and the refugees, who were skeptical of our motives and our claims that we had their best interests at heart. "What do you know about the LGBT community?" one person demanded. I told them I was gay, and they burst into applause. OK, they all said, come talk to us.

Inge De Langhe, the senior protection officer at UNHCR who works closely with the LGBT refugees at Kakuma, had introduced us to these refugees. In the camp, the LGBT refugees, in this case all from Uganda, had been grouped together into a few small compounds to make it easier to monitor their safety. This had mixed effects in practice— other refugees who wished them ill knew where they lived, and in at least one case, set fire to their encampment, but the LGBT communities within the compounds could count on one another for security. As one Ugandan explained to us, even if they had been living separately, there was no way to live under the radar; since there is no war or ongoing crisis in Uganda, it was generally assumed in Kakuma that to be Ugandan was to be gay.

Still, the refugees stressed concern for their safety and the safety of those who remained in the countries they had fled. Within the compounds we could speak openly, but often they asked that their identities be obscured or faces hidden, and that we use their first initial or a nickname. Outside of Kakuma, interviews took place behind closed doors if their living spaces were secure, or in public places that were away from prying ears, such as a park in the middle of Nairobi.

At a time when LGBT rights are in the news as never before, there is a large and growing appetite for stories about the LGBT experience in places such as Kenya, where the danger is acute and previously reported stories are scarce and often lack depth. The LGBT journalists have a real opportunity to create deep and meaningful coverage that is informed by their lived experiences.

But being an LGBT journalist has its disadvantages, too. A gay photographer based in the Middle East, who is working on a long-term project about LGBT refugees from countries in the region where homophobia is deeply entrenched, told me that although his sexuality has made it easier to get close to his subjects, it has also put him at risk.

"Of course, once the interviewee or subject of the photograph realizes the interviewer or photographer is somehow connected to them in terms of being LGBT, it automatically breaks down the barriers. There's an added comfort factor when people realize you're also gay," said the photographer, who asked to remain anonymous due to security concerns. But he also worries about being a target himself. Though he would love to pursue this project in Iraq, he doesn't think it would be safe for anyone involved. "The idea of doing something LGBT-related there makes me very fearful both for myself and my subject."

His Middle East project began with documenting LGBT Iraqis fleeing persecution and seeking refuge in Syria. Though there were risks (a Westerner photographing Iraqis in Syria drew unwanted attention), he says it wasn't too difficult to find his way into the community. The real challenge was balancing safety with the need to make the most compelling image possible. "It's a compromise between them understanding that you would like to take a photo that says something about their personality and their situation, but also something that you both feel respects them," he said.

Recently, with the rise of the Islamic State group, his ability to pursue this and similar projects in the region has been greatly restricted, both out of fear for his subjects and, increasingly, for his own safety. He has turned down assignments in areas where he is worried that his sexuality might make him a target, and takes security precautions, such as carrying around a photograph of a fake girlfriend and being discreet about what he shares on social media.

During my reporting process in Kenya, I interviewed a fringe right-wing politician who introduced a bill in that country's parliament that called for the stoning to death of "local gays," and he told me that Western gays that come to Kenya and promote homosexuality should also be killed. As we sat in a café in downtown Nairobi, he went on and on about how much the gays deserved death, not knowing that I was gay. Though I didn't feel seriously at risk, it was yet another strong reminder that people in many countries across the world wish people like me harm.

Though everyone with whom I spoke talked about the ways identifying as LGBT made at least parts of the reporting process easier and knew the risks it posed, some were quick to point out that it also comes with other challenges beyond immediate risk. From an editorial perspective, Selly Thiam felt she was perceived as being unable to produce quality, unbiased reporting about LGBT issues. Thiam is a Senegalese lesbian journalist and activist who works in Kenya and identifies as a member of the African diaspora. Earlier in her career, while working as a journalist in the U.S., she recalled pitching stories on Africa or queer issues and being told she couldn't be objective, then having editors ask her to write stories about deadbeat dads in the black community. "It's important that as journalists we complicate this idea of who can report what stories and that we complicate the idea that just because we are part of a community we can't do our jobs properly, which is not true," Thiam said.

She runs the oral history project None on Record, which began as a documentary project about LGBT Africans in the diaspora. Since then, it has evolved into a media advocacy group, producing its own documentaries, doing sensitivity training for local journalists, and bringing local LGBT people into the mainstream conversation in a variety of ways.

But Thiam also cautions against assuming too many commonalities because of a shared LGBT identity. "Definitely when people know that you identify as LGBT, particularly working in communities on the continent, it makes things a bit easier, but then there's all these other things that come after that, like class, nationality, educational status, access to resources, language; there are just so many other things that make up a person, including their sexuality," she said. Her point is that sexuality may help a reporter clear one hurdle, but many other barriers remain in forging a meaningful connection with a source, or in understanding their lived experiences with any nuance.

Thiam is entrenched in the communities where she works and is particularly concerned that people who parachute in—LGBT-identifying or not—without thinking about the safety of their subjects can do real harm. "The assumption that just because we're all queer then we're all gonna get along and get each other is just not … It can be dangerous. There have been queer journalists that have come in to do stories in Uganda and Kenya who have done more harm than good, because they think they know."

■ ■ ■

Jake Naughton is a New York-based journalist focusing on LGBT and immigration issues. He contributes to The New York Times *and his work has appeared in outlets including* Al Jazeera America, Newsweek, *and* GlobalPost.

6. The Progression of Hate

By Michelle Ferrier

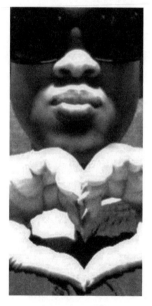

Michelle Ferrier illustrates her efforts to combat online harassment using positive messaging, love and "an anonymous face."

Source: Michelle Ferrier

Even today, the words scribbled across the pages in angry ALL CAPS are hard to look at.

"HOW DO YOU GET A NIGGER OUT OF A TREE? CUT THE ROPE!!"

"BEFORE THIS WORLD ENDS, THERE WILL BE A RACE WAR ..."

"ALL YOU PEOPLE DO IS CRY BITCH WINE [sic], BITCH."

"HAVE YOU PLAYED THE RACE CARD MICHELLE THIS WEEK?"

Back then, I would pull the letters I received out of sealed plastic bags with rubber gloves while standing outdoors, so as not to expose my co-workers at the newspaper to any potential toxins—and to preserve any fingerprints that might still be imprinted atop these hateful words.

I would stare at the manifestos—some of which were several pages long, and others scrawled across clippings of newspaper articles from across the southeastern seaboard—directed at me, mailed to the newsroom every few months between 2005 and 2007. They were little written terrorist bombs tossed into my daily routine of getting my children off to school, studying in my graduate program and working at Florida's *Daytona Beach News-Journal* as a night news editor, weekly columnist and online community manager. It was my role as a columnist that made me a target for hate letters.

The comments were included in anonymous letters and envelopes with no return address. As the first African-American columnist at the newspaper, I wrote a weekly lifestyle column called "Chasing Rainbows" for more than five years and my picture appeared next to those columns.

I wrote slice-of-life columns, personal fly-on-the-wall accounts of life in an African-American household with young children. I wrote about teaching my children to ride bicycles, the Halloween costumes we made, our reactions to world events as they unfolded before us. My first column painfully asked how to explain death to young children as we watched the horror of the Columbia shuttle explosion playing over and over on our television screen in 2003. Subsequent columns illuminated intimate spaces of the African-American experience that were as universal as any other story. My last column celebrated Barack Obama's inauguration as the 44th president of the United States.

Each column represented a personal narrative of my everyday life intended to resonate across gender, ethnic, age or other categorizations of my readers. I shared my family's intimate moments to try to bridge differences. And the stories connected with many readers in the Daytona Beach audience of transplants, locals, snowbirds, retirees, young families and others. I often spoke at public schools, civic events, church services and other venues about writing, my columns and my readers' responses.

My column coincided with the rise of "mommy bloggers" in the online world. We were the vanguard, moving our lifestyle columns from printed newspapers onto online platforms that received worldwide visibility. However, just as in the physical world, hate and misogyny moved online. Women writers found themselves at the forefront of uncovering just how ugly anonymous Web audiences can be.

When I received the first anonymous letter, I realized there was a dark undercurrent to my audience. The big, block letters shouted vitriol from the page. One, in particular, stood out—a lengthy diatribe, full of hateful imagery designed to strike terror. I couldn't understand how someone could hate so much, and direct that hate toward me, a person he or she had encountered only through a picture and a column in a newspaper. I shoved the letter into a folder for my special fan mail ... the kind that made my skin crawl.

■ ■ ■

In addition to writing as a columnist for the newspaper, I worked the night news desk, often arriving to work at 5 p.m. and completing my shift at 1:30 a.m. My husband worked a few blocks from my building and I would drop off the kids with him on my way to work. He would drive them home, get them dinner and put them to bed.

I worked in the newsroom with a skeleton crew of 20 employees in the building, deep into the night, editing local copy, designing pages and proofing the paper before it went to press. There was no security at the building after midnight and I often walked through the darkness to my car alone.

Only after receiving several angry letters did I finally go to the police. By this time, my husband and I had an alarm system installed in our home. I had begun asking colleagues about their experiences with hate mail and other reader reactions. I called professional organizations to discuss what resources were available for members who experienced this type of harassment. I asked the Federal Bureau of Investigation (FBI), local law enforcement, the Florida Department of Law Enforcement and other agencies and professional organizations to investigate my case.

Usually, I got a shrug. Some journalism colleagues considered hate mail a badge of honor. They must be doing something right, they reasoned, to prompt such a visceral response. The typical response from the professional organizations I contacted was, "We don't have anything to deal with that."

On the law enforcement side, my conversations weren't much more fruitful. Basically, I was told, "There's nothing we can do" because this letter writer hadn't fulfilled his threats; these were just threats. Hate mail, it seemed, could not really be investigated until something actually happened. Until whoever this was actually did something to me, there was nothing the authorities could do.

I had literally put my life into my columns. Community members knew my children's names, where they went to school, how they were doing on their school projects and their obsessions with video games and reading. How could I protect them from this nameless, faceless threat?

I certainly tried. I wasn't going to leave my life or the lives of my children in such cavalier hands. I researched laws and tracked down legal cases, and eventually found sympathetic ears at the Southern Poverty Law Center, whose staff researches incidents of hate crimes across the United States. I reiterated my suspicions about the letters—that this wasn't the work of one racist, crazy person. This letter-writing campaign was a coordinated effort, a tactic used by hate groups to shut down diverse voices through intimidation and fear.

When the letters kept coming, I finally convinced the police to set up a special patrol around my neighborhood. Our children had cell phones long before their peers, so they could communicate with my husband and me at all times. I had begun wearing wigs and disguising myself when I went about in public, and I began to avoid making public appearances. I never talked about the letters in my columns, fearing that to mention the horrible threats might cause them to escalate.

■ ■ ■

Unless it has happened to you, it is hard to imagine what this kind of stalking feels like. Trust me. You don't want to know. Even years later, thinking, talking or writing about these experiences makes it hard for me to breathe.

I felt powerless. I became more suspicious. I was frustrated. I had a voice, a platform to talk about issues, but I couldn't talk about this. The cowards could not even face me, would not participate in any sort of dialogue with me, would not allow me to challenge their stereotypes of black people. I struggled to remain authentic to my readers as I kept this shadow side of my life out of the newspaper.

My newspaper management created a protocol to handle my mail. When a suspicious letter came to the building, it would be bagged and sent to Human Resources, who would call me. I would carefully carry the bag to the local police department for copies and to add to my unresolved report. At night, management suggested I walk with a co-worker to my car to keep me safe. As the letters continued, these procedures seemed pointless. Months turned into years.

I became a different person as a result of my hate mail. I became less trusting. I had always naively thought that I would be willing to die rather than have to kill someone. But as the letters continued, I became angrier. I learned to shoot a gun. I was prepared physically and mentally to defend my family and myself. Each day, I would take a different route to and from work, trying to outsmart the crazy.

You would think that this could be something one could get used to, that maybe, over time, it would become easier to read each successive letter. But letters turned to packages. White supremacist newsletters sent to me became the backing for ever-escalating hate. And toward the end, I couldn't recognize what little humanity might be lurking behind each envelope. I had become the target of every bad thing that had happened in this letter writer's life and the lives of white people. And he wanted me to pay ... in the upcoming race wars featuring me and all the other niggers.

It didn't help that as the rhetoric heated up, a black man was rising in power. In fact, the Southern Poverty Law Center pointed to a spike in hate crimes nationwide and written attacks against Obama leading up to the inauguration. Finally, the Committee to Protect Journalists heard of my case. They followed up with the FBI, retrieved copies of the letters and in 2008 wrote to the U.S. Department of Justice, asking for an investigation. The response: Nothing. We now had a black president and it seemed that all the hate groups were whipped into a frenzy. My case was no doubt dwarfed by the efforts to protect our first black president.

I shied away from controversial topics in my columns, attempting to use a keyboard like a divining rod to see what might provoke a racist response. I became contemplative, thinking out loud with my readers about my family and wrestling with difficult life choices. My readers knew me too well. After all, when you open your heart as I did each week, readers will recognize when things are off. One day, a long-time reader called me in the newsroom. "I know something's going on and I'm not going to let you off the phone until you tell me," she demanded. "I've been reading your last couple of columns and something's going on. Can I help?"

I broke down and told her about the letters. Outside of my employer and the law enforcement agencies, I hadn't shared with friends or family what was going on. But her genuine desire to help broke through the defenses I'd built against the outside world and my own readers.

She offered her home as a safe house. She gave me her phone number and told me where to find the spare key so I could let myself in. "Don't stop writing. That would let them win," she said.

I kept writing. But the emotional strain on my family and me was taking its toll. My children sensed something was going on. Every time a letter arrived at the newspaper, Mommy was even more vigilant, requiring check-ins at school, at home and with friends. The police patrols would increase and then die down again. I stopped working on the night news desk and moved into a new daytime position as an online community manager. I kept writing, while wondering if it was worth it.

Someone wanted to silence my voice. Intellectually, I could understand why. Those homespun stories were making a difference. One column I wrote about a field trip with my daughter to a plantation prompted one reader to admit his African-American heritage—and pledge to invite his black relatives to the next family reunion. The story I wrote about losing our family cat prompted an avalanche of mail from readers sharing their grief. Being a columnist was more than an intellectual activity or a job—it was a mission to connect us as humans, despite our differences. My columns reflected the experiences of one African-American family and our everyday struggles. It was my heart, served up weekly. However, inside, I was bleeding from these anonymous, racist cuts. Just as I would think things had died down, BAM! Another paper cut to the heart.

The next letter I received was the last straw. I remember getting it from Human Resources and the chagrined look on my co-worker's face as I recognized the handwriting on the envelope. Driving down the street to the police station, I pulled over and read the letter, plastic gloves wiping away the tears as the hate screamed up from the page.

A mantra kept repeating in my head: *I don't have to live like this. I don't have to live like this. I don't have to live like this.* I called my husband to say that I was taking another letter to the police. And that this was the last one. I was done. I was leaving the newspaper.

My next call was to my boss. "I'm resigning," I said. "I can't do this anymore."

I didn't say goodbye to my readers, though I knew as I wrote my last column about Obama's inauguration that it was going to be my last. There's hopefulness embedded in my words, for black people, for an America that finally moved past race and elected a black president, for race relations in general. There's hopefulness for a post-racial America that the reality of my life mocked. I still dreamed of something different. I wanted something different for me and for my children and for my country. However, as the column went to press, I was on my way to a new job as a journalism professor in a state far, far away.

■ ■ ■

There are long-term psychological impacts to the type of hate I experienced. You never forget. When #gamergate began attacking female journalists online in August 2014, I remembered my own experiences and wanted to do something "anti-gamergate" to help the targets of online harassment persist online. These online trolls have used social media to swarm female journalists and thought leaders, damaging our identities, our digital reputations and our ability to make a living. Women are most at risk online, particularly female journalists.

I know.

That's why in January 2015, I founded TrollBusters (www.troll-busters.com)—a just-in-time rescue service for female journalists. We provide a hedge of protection around women so they can persist online and tell the story, and not become the story.

■ ■ ■

Michelle Ferrier worked for the Daytona Beach News-Journal *from 2002 to 2009, during which she completed her Ph.D. program in texts and technology and pioneered emerging technologies in online communities, online learning and virtual reality. She is the founder of TrollBusters, a service and technology to support female journalists against online harassment.*

7. Double Exposure

By Jessica Jerreat

Uganda's LGBT community is using journalism to try to counter negative reporting after the tabloid *Red Pepper*, pictured, published a list of what it called the country's "200 top homosexuals."

Source: AP/Stephen Wandera

W hen it comes to abusive readers' comments and tweets from Internet trolls, Katherine O'Donnell has heard it all. For years, O'Donnell, who is night editor of the Scottish edition of the U.K.'s *The Times*, has borne the brunt of personal attacks, including about her gender, from online trolls who take umbrage at articles in her newspaper.

"They say never read below the line," O'Donnell said in an October 2015 email. "My Twitter feed has its share of blocked trolls, including a host of cybernats [Scottish nationalist extremists] who have not been shy in denigrating my trans status when castigating me for the views expressed in *The Times*."

For the most part O'Donnell, who has worked at *The Times* for more than 12 years, shrugs off the comments, saying, "I'm not a spokeswoman for trans people. I'm a journalist who happens to be trans."

The U.K. is at the more tolerant end of the spectrum regarding gender status, and most conflicts affecting transgender people typically include anonymous online attacks, discrimination or lack of sensitivity among peers or in the way the subject is reported in the press. But even in the U.K., violence is sometimes directed toward transgender people. At the more dangerous end of the spectrum are countries like Uganda, where narrow views of sex and gender status are rigidly enforced by the government and violence is a greater risk, making it harder for transgender people to shrug off verbal or online attacks.

Advocacy groups[1] tracking conditions in Uganda have reported on attacks,[2] sexual violence and, in some cases, legal action against transgender people. Victims of gender-related crimes often do not report the attacks to authorities for fear of legal action and further harassment. Members of the LGBTI (lesbian, gay, bisexual, transgender and intersex) community in Uganda also face the threat of violence after being publicly outed, as happened in February 2014, when two people were reported[3] to have been attacked after the newspaper *Red Pepper* published a list of "200 top homosexuals" under the headline "Exposed."

For Uganda's press, reporting on transgender issues can also lead to charges of "promoting homosexuality." An anti-homosexuality law under which gays could face life imprisonment was repealed in 2014, but a draft law[4] set to replace it threatens seven-year jail terms for the "promotion of homosexuality."

Among gender issues, transexualism is at the forefront of changing mores around the world, sometimes with dangerous implications, including for journalists. Despite the risks of legal action or physical attacks, many journalists insist on covering related issues in Uganda. The people behind *Kuchu Times*, an outlet set up to provide a platform[5] for LGBTI voices and to try to counter negative reporting in the mainstream press, say they are determined to take on ill-informed views. The outlet regularly features either accounts from transgender contributors about their experiences or news about violence and discrimination against transgender and gay people, through its news website and online radio and television station. Some of the contributors and staff use pseudonyms[6] to protect them from prosecution under Uganda's anti-gay laws.

"Discrimination is our lived reality," said a staff member and contributor to *Kuchu Times* who asked to be identified only as Ruth M. "However, this hasn't stopped our reporters from ensuring that stories from the transgender and LGB family are heard. Transphobia is an issue that we as an LGBTI community continue to struggle with—hence our trans-identifying reporters continue to face stigma and discrimination in their work."

Due to the risk of attacks, only a few have access to the studio that the outlet uses for its online broadcasts, and the reporters and contributors, especially those who are transgender, are advised to take extra precautions while working, Ruth M. said, adding, "We operate in an already hostile and biased environment."

There is reason to be cautious. Uganda is one of more than 30 African countries[7] where being gay is criminalized, and although transgender people are not always gay, they often fall under discriminatory legislation.

Violence and threats against this group can also lead to murder. Between 2008 and September 2015, 1,933 murders of transgender and gender-variant (not identifying as either male or female) people were reported worldwide, with nine victims killed in African countries, including two in Uganda, according to the Berlin-based regional organization Transgender Europe, whose ongoing research project on Trans Murder Monitoring[8] tracks the deaths of transgender people globally. The results of this monitoring project show that in the U.K. during the same period, seven transgender people were murdered, including one in 2015. The country with the highest figure was Brazil, with more than 770 reported murders.

Kikonyogo Kivumbi, executive director of Uganda Health and Science Press Association, described transgender people as "a minority within a minority" and said, "There is little understanding in Uganda about trans people." According to Kivumbi, journalists writing about transgender issues "receive reprisal, reaction, [and are] undermined by editors and fellow staff because many people in Uganda believe all trans people are gay."

Journalists in more liberal countries, such as the U.K., face a different array of threats, but even there not everyone is inured to the lack of understanding or the vitriol on social media and in online comments. Jennie Kermode, chair of London-based Trans Media Watch, said that although she is not aware of any cases in the U.K., where a threat made on Twitter led to an assault, fear remains.

Mainstream news outlets in the U.K. are giving more prominent space to transgender issues, and transgender reporters are assuming more visible roles. Yet even in the U.K., reporters who cover the subject, or who happen to be transgender, may find themselves the focus of cruel and abusive comments, including from fellow journalists. Often, they also have to deal with sensational reporting.

"Over the last year, there have been some frankly abysmal blunders around the reporting of trans people," O'Donnell said. Some news outlets, including the *New Statesman*,[9] *Daily Mail* and *The Spectator*,[10] have "devoted a lot of space, and sometimes, gleefully, to the activities and views of TERFs [trans-exclusionary radical feminists], who are dedicated to making the lives of trans people even more difficult," she said.

In discussing these issues in the U.K., many journalists and advocates bring up columnist Julie Burchill, whose work has been featured in several national newspapers, including *The Spectator* and *The Sunday Times*, as someone who has written negatively about the transgender community. In March 2014, Burchill sparked angry debate after she left abusive comments under an article that journalist Paris Lees wrote for *Vice* magazine about enjoying the attention of men on the street. The comments, which included crude remarks about Lees and about gender reassignment surgery, and the claim that only humans born female can refer to themselves as women, were later deleted, according to *Pink News*,[11] which covers LGBTI issues and reported that Burchill added an apology that was also later deleted.

Burchill did not respond to emailed requests for comment, forwarded to her by her book publisher and sent through news outlets to which she contributes, about the Paris Lees incident and claims that online harassment from a fellow journalist could deter transgender reporters.

Critics say such behavior has the potential to undermine growing sensitivity to gender issues in the mainstream British press and the work of organizations such as media groups All About Trans and Trans Media Watch to ensure fairer reporting on transgender people.

Kermode said getting editors to recognize the problem of such attacks is crucial to changing the media's approach to transgender reporting. "While we are very much in favor of freedom of speech and would not object, for instance, to speculation on why people are trans—though for the sake of quality journalism, we'd hope there was some science involved in the argument, we hope people will see that attacks intended to insult or stir up hatred are just as damaging when made against trans people as they are when made against a specific racial or religious group," Kermode said.

Groups such as Trans Media Watch say one way to counter such abuse is to reduce the unnecessary focus of news reports on an irrelevant transgender angle. O'Donnell, who shares that view, cited as an example news reports about an academic who nearly died after being gored by a stag as she walked home in the Scottish Highlands. "An unprovoked attack by a large wild beast is a solid story by any standard, but several papers were obsessed with the fact that the victim was trans, as if it was somehow pertinent to the attack," O'Donnell said. "As I pointed out, forcefully but fruitlessly, as it happened, we would not consider it to be germane if the victim was Jewish, or Asian, or gay, so why would we report that she is trans?"

When the victim recovered, she lodged a complaint with the Press Complaints Commission, a regulatory media body in the U.K. The commission found that six U.K. national newspapers—the *Daily Mail, The Sun, Daily Telegraph, The Scottish Sun,* the *Daily Mirror* and the *Daily Record*—had breached the discriminatory clause of the commission's code through their headlines in May 2014. The newspapers agreed to amend the online versions of the stories, according to the BBC.[12]

The Press Complaints Commission and anti-discrimination laws provide protective measures in the U.K., and All About Trans and Trans Media Watch both actively promote increasing transgender voices in the media and offer advice on how to report sensitively and on dealing with harassment. But in Uganda, laws, including those directed at the media, enable repression or actively persecute the LGBTI community.

Press freedom is already limited in Uganda and journalists of any gender face danger even from those who might be expected to protect them. As the Committee to Protect Journalists has reported,[13] critical news outlets in the country have been suspended and police have been implicated in assaults on journalists. In October 2015, human rights watchdog Privacy International reported that the Ugandan government had bought and used FinFisher surveillance software "to spy on leading opposition members, activists, elected officials, intelligence insiders and journalists following the 2011 election, which President Museveni [won] following evidence of vote-buying and misuse of state funds."

Coupled with this heavy-handed approach to a critical media are Uganda's draconian laws affecting the LGBTI community. Colin Stewart, editor and publisher at the international advocacy group Erasing 76 Crimes, which challenges repressive anti-gay legislation, said that anti-LGBTI violence is "distressingly common" in Uganda and in numerous other countries as well, including Jamaica, Cameroon, Kenya, Nigeria and Sierra Leone. "Citizens of every country with repressive laws need to learn about the inhumane effects of their country's anti-LGBTI laws, stigmatization, repression, and discrimination. *Kuchu Times* does that well for Ugandans."

Ruth M., of *Kuchu Times*, acknowledged that the group has had some success. "[Our] platform is currently attracting many visitors, even the anti-gay groups involved, which we hope will help them to learn something about the struggles of LGBTI people and communities in the hope to create attitude change," she said. By sharing their accounts, the columnists featured in *Kuchu Times* and on other media platforms hope to create greater empathy and understanding.

Erasing 76 Crimes also uses reporting to inform others of the harmful effects of anti-gay legislation. "We inform people worldwide and, at the same time, provide a media outlet for local activists who are excluded from coverage by homophobic local media," Stewart said. "Individual stories are a powerful tool that can encourage disempowered sexual minorities to recognize their own worth."

An example of this kind of proactive reporting is an account by Beyonce Karungi published by *Kuchu Times* on September 15, 2015,[14] in which she detailed how she had been rejected by her family and felt compelled to turn to sex work to support herself. Alleged harassment by authorities, including an incident in which she says police humiliated her and forced her to "cut my hair to make me look more masculine," made her not feel safe enough to report being raped.

To amplify the voices of the LGBTI community, *Kuchu Times* publishes *Bombastic Magazine*, the first edition of which was distributed across the country in late 2014 with copies also sent to politicians and other key figures, according to Agence France-Presse.[15] Some volunteer distributors in western Uganda reported that they were threatened, and some copies were burned in the country's eastern region, Agence France-Presse[16] reported.

Ruth M. said that despite its successes, the news outlet struggles to find adequate financial backing. "Local funding is impossible, and we thus have to depend on foreign donations, which don't come easily," she said. "Time and again our website and publication *Bombastic Magazine* have been branded as recruitment tools for homosexuality. This has escalated censorship by authorities into our work."

Part of Uganda's draft law to prohibit "promoting homosexuality" is a proposed ban on "funding for purposes of promoting unnatural sexual practices."[17] To avoid such a conflict, *Kuchu Times* used crowdsourcing to raise money for the second issue of *Bombastic*, scheduled for distribution in January 2016. The outlet reports that its IndieGogo campaign exceeded its $5,000 goal, and by early November 2015 had brought in more than $8,300.

In the U.K., transgender journalists sometimes face problems of stereotyping, Kermode said. "It's very difficult for them to get work writing about anything other than trans issues," she said, adding, "they all report receiving a lot of personal abuse. This seems, anecdotally, to be worse for the women, so we suspect it's compounded by misogyny." Some aspiring transgender reporters are put off by what they consider to be hostile newsrooms, she said.

When Trans Media Watch began operations in 2010, the organization had difficulty finding journalists willing to talk openly about their
experiences, Kermode said. "There was a fear of personal attacks and
also a fear of being monstered by newspapers, a phenomenon that was
quite common at the time. Some of us worked in journalism but simply didn't publish anything about trans issues or about those aspects of
our own lives, while other people felt simply they could never enter
the profession."

O'Donnell, who was late night editor at *The Times* when she transitioned, said that in her view, "newsrooms are cruel environments and
journalists are not always generous." When she began at *The Times*,
O'Donnell said she found herself quickly promoted. Within a year of
starting work there, she was responsible for editing two nightly edi-
tions, and when she transitioned, she had the "immediate and unam-
biguous support" of then-editor Robert Thomson and his deputy, Ben
Preston, she said. O'Donnell was also invited to rewrite the paper's
style guide entry for trans people. "A majority of my colleagues, but
not all, were thoughtful and kind, if not always entirely understanding," O'Donnell said. "There were some bad-taste jokes and unpleas-
ant things said, but the transition itself was less difficult than I had
anticipated.

"It was only long after the dust had settled that I began to realize
that my career path would come up against active resistance in some
quarters and that acceptance and equality was very much conditional,"
O'Donnell said. "It's a work situation that many, many women will
recognize."

O'Donnell said her experience has made her more outspoken. "I
have intervened with colleagues whenever I have seen trans people or
issues reported inaccurately or unfairly," she said. "I doubt that this has
made me especially popular but to their credit, generally I have been
listened to."

Finding support for sensitive reporting is also a challenge for
Ugandan journalists. Kivumbi, of the Uganda Health and Science Press
Association, said that journalists in the country often have problems
finding outlets willing to run their stories. "It's not easy for an editor
to pass a trans people story or interview in mainstream media," she said.
"What the anti-gay forces have done is to infiltrate and promote hate

as part of the internal editorial or broadcast policy in many newsrooms in Uganda."

Still, Kivumbi added, "Such news channels like *Kuchu Times* demystify the hate."

Often hostility toward the transgender community takes the form of online attacks, which is the most pervasive threat in the U.K. Moderators of British news sites are responsible for monitoring hate speech in readers' comments, and owners of social media accounts have the option of blocking trolls or reporting abuse. In May 2015, *The Telegraph*[18] reported that Twitter had been asked to block an account by someone impersonating an Australian feminist, and who had paid to have their tweets urging transgender people to kill themselves to be promoted on users' feeds. A spokesman for Twitter told *The Telegraph* that the social network bans hate speech and, "As soon as we were made aware we removed the [promoted post] and suspended the account."

Kermode said her group would like social media groups to take stronger action to prevent or interrupt attacks. "There is a problem on Twitter whereby if one simply blocks somebody one can still see that person's tweets when they're forwarded by other people," she said. "Some people are afraid of not reading hostile tweets because they want to be alert to situations which could spill over into real life. It's not uncommon for threats of physical violence to be made. It takes a certain toughness to keep working despite this."

■ ■ ■

Jessica Jerreat is CPJ's senior editor, responsible for special reports, including "Balancing Act: Press Freedom at Risk as EU Struggles to Match Action With Values" and "Drawing the Line: Cartoonists Under Threat." She previously edited news for the broadsheet press in the United Kingdom, including The Telegraph *and the foreign desk of* The Times. *She has a master's degree in war, propaganda and society from the University of Kent in Canterbury.*

8. Combating Digital Harassment

By Dunja Mijatović

The OSCE's representative on freedom of the media was shocked by the number and nature of threats that female journalists reported having experienced on a daily basis.

Source: OSCE/Micky Kroell

A plurality of online voices is good for democracy, yet one group has come under attack in the most gruesome ways. Threats of rape, physical violence and graphic imagery are showing up in the inboxes and on the social media platforms of female journalists across the globe. Though online harassment of journalists is not new, it has become a particular cause for concern and a deterrent to free expression for many female journalists who have made valuable contributions to the news. I have had the privilege to work with many of them.

In February 2015, the Office of the Representative on Freedom of the Media, with the Organization for Security and Co-operation in Europe (OSCE), undertook a qualitative survey to begin taking stock of the prevalence of online harassment of female journalists in participating states. I am the official representative on freedom of the media, and for all of us, the responses we received were a wake-up call, truly shocking in terms of the number and nature of threats most of the women had experienced on a daily basis.

For the sake of brevity, and out of sensitivity to those who have been subjected to such abuse, I will reduce the prevalent message that was being delivered to the journalists this way: "Women who talk too much need to get raped." The gender component of this harassment is clear, rearing its ugly head in the type of threats and language used, which goes beyond traditional vitriol to employ threats of rape and graphic (often sexual) violence with the aim of silencing women online. Though these journalists were attacked both as journalists and as women, this is not merely a "women's issue." Limiting the diversity of voices online hurts everyone, and without the recognition of men and their engagement in combating the attacks, little can be done to stop it.

Women who face this type of harassment have little recourse when it comes to reporting on this type of abuse in a way that will likely produce results, or receive support or legal redress. At best, they are encouraged to ignore the abuse and turn off the computer, and at worst, are blamed for the abuse or for undermining others' free speech. Obviously, turning off the computer is not an acceptable or realistic solution. While the vitriol may be limited to the virtual world, the threat to women's safety and reputation is real. In fact, many journalists claim that the very nature of the Internet—which enables complete anonymity and total access to information, including social, personal and financial data—makes it impossible to escape aggressors and multiplies the harmful effects of online harassment. One journalist who responded to our survey wrote, "When I go to the frontline, I choose to go and put myself ... in a hostile environment. To feel this psychological stress in my house only because I give my opinion on Twitter or Facebook, it's unbearable." It is worth noting that this came from a war correspondent.

Among those surveyed, 95 percent confirmed that the vast majority of the work-related threats and harassment they face takes place online. But the same factors that make it difficult for them to avoid harassment also stymie efforts by law enforcement and government officials to effectively punish those responsible or to prevent the online attacks from occurring. The main problem is that the attacks are amorphous and transitory. There is also a lack of concrete data. For policymakers who want to have a real impact in bolstering female journalists' safety online, the collection of data, including specific instances of online abuse and the quantitative and qualitative effects on the journalists' work (both online and offline), would be a key first step.

Also lacking are industry-wide standards on what constitutes hate speech and specific thresholds for restrictions. Journalists need to be able to name and catalogue such abuses, and these standards cannot be set arbitrarily. They will require the input of all stakeholders, including members of civil society, intermediaries, media outlets, international organizations and journalists.

To begin this process at the Office of the Representative on Freedom of the Media, we used the findings from our survey together with preliminary recommendations that were laid out in our "Communiqué 02/2015 on the Growing Safety Threat to Female Journalists Online"[1] to put together a forum on the issue in September 2015.

Media experts, representatives of Internet intermediary companies, members of the public and government policymakers from OSCE participating state governments who attended the forum discussed the obstacles that each group of stakeholders faces as well as realistic opportunities for countering online harassment. The meeting enabled journalists to talk directly with policymakers about their personal experiences with online harassment, thus framing the debate in the reality of female journalists' everyday lives, and about the consequences of such abuse, the differences and shared experiences across national borders, and the ways in which they were able to seek support and recourse.

From this discussion, a more comprehensive understanding about the prevalence of this type of abuse took shape. Although the repercussions of online harassment are exacerbated in countries where democratic principles, such as freedom of expression, already suffer, testimony from journalists at the conference confirmed that the problem occurs throughout the OSCE region, as well as in other parts of the world. Caroline Criado-Perez, a U.K. journalist who has been outspoken about the pervasive harassment she has faced since 2013, shocked the gathering by reading aloud some of the disturbing and graphic threats she has received. Azerbaijani journalist Arzu Geybullayeva told forum participants that she has received several death threats and numerous messages threatening the safety of her and her family. Both women have had their home addresses published online, accompanied by threats of rape and physical violence.

Many of the journalists present at the conference spoke about the lack of necessary law enforcement tools and understanding of technology to effectively protect victims. With technology constantly changing, the ways in which journalists are attacked are also evolving, and today include the posting of revenge porn, cyber-mobbing and denial-of-service attacks. A consensus among those who attended the forum was that digital literacy should be included in comprehensive training for law enforcement officials to ensure that victims get the support they need and that the perpetrators are thwarted—in the best case, before they launch an attack. Law enforcement officials need data on the motivations behind such attacks, ready access to information on legal precedents, and a clear definition of what constitutes a digital hate crime.

The meeting represented the beginning of what I hope will be a long-term focus on this issue at the OSCE and other international organizations. Afterward, my office released a list of specific recommendations[2] for policymakers on how best to ensure that existing legal frameworks are used effectively to support female journalists who are subject to online harassment, including the following:

- Strengthen the capacity of law enforcement agencies to understand international standards on human rights so they can identify real threats to safety and protect individuals in danger, including providing tools and training on technical and legal issues.
- Commission and support the collection and analysis of data related to online abuse and its effects, including creating a database of specific occurrences and follow-up from law enforcement.
- Establish a network of working groups with participating states, international organizations, media, civil society and Internet intermediaries to develop educational materials and awareness-raising campaigns and create effective structures for dialogue.
- Recognize that threats and other forms of online abuse of female journalists and media actors are a direct attack on freedom of expression and freedom of the media.

These crucial steps would provide law enforcement agencies the tools to better identify these types of crimes and to provide real protection for victims within international legal frameworks.

One of the most important, though less understood, points is that we already have the necessary legal framework to successfully curtail this devastating trend. That framework includes the Universal Declaration of Human Rights, the International Convention on Civil and Political Rights, the U.N. Convention on the Elimination of All Forms of Discrimination Against Women, the Beijing Platform for Action, the U.N. Plan of Action on Safety of Journalists and the Issue of Impunity, and a number of U.N. resolutions, including L13 on Internet Free Speech. Together, these measures provide an overarching framework for ensuring that female journalists can freely work. The key is not to introduce new legislation that could have the negative effect of stifling freedom of expression, but to provide the information and resources to effectively use existing legislation to protect journalists' safety and put an end to gender-based discrimination.

Online abuse endangers media pluralism and democracy as a whole. According to one report,[3] only 24 percent of people working in print, radio and television news are female. If this type of harassment is left unchecked, it could result in self-censorship by female journalists and diminished female perspective online.

One war correspondent who has suffered repeated online harassment explained in her response to the survey that she had taken time away from her work. "I needed the break," she wrote. "But it's made me think if it's really worth it, to cover Israel and Palestine." The bottom line is simple: Policymakers at every level and in every sector must make it a high priority to ensure that journalists of any gender can work freely and without fear of online harassment, which is a direct attack on our fundamental freedoms.

■ ■ ■

Dunja Mijatović is representative on freedom of the media, a position to which she was appointed in 2010 by the Ministerial Council of the Organization for Security and Co-operation in Europe, which carries a political mandate to protect and promote freedom of expression and freedom of the media in the 57 participating states.

9. Responding to Internet Abuse

By Courtney C. Radsch

Journalists facing online threats are often told to stay off social media, but most in the profession consider this impractical.

Source: Reuters/Albert Gea

A na Freitas, a 26-year-old Brazilian journalist who covers pop culture, recalled how she once had trouble convincing an editor at the news outlet *YouPix* to publish an article she had written about women and minorities being unwelcome on comment boards related to pop cultural videos, movies, comics or gaming.

At the time, Freitas was a freelancer, and although the editor praised the quality of the article, the newspaper declined to publish it. "They didn't want that type of attention," she said during a session about violence against women online at the Internet Governance Forum in João Pessoa, Brazil in November 2015.

Freitas said she ended up publishing the article on *HuffPost Brasil*[1] and immediately received vicious threats on social media. Her personal information was put online, known as doxxing, and she received packages filled with worms at her house. She left home for several weeks out of fear for her and her family's safety.

Among the repercussions of the online attacks was that editors stopped accepting her work. "I can't work as a freelancer anymore," she told me. The online attackers stripped her of that livelihood.

"It would be great if during this process of rethinking their role in society, the media companies realize it is really, really essential that they back up the people working for them, whether they are freelancers or not," she said.

After giving up freelancing, Freitas began working as a staff writer. She now writes for *Nexo Jornal*, and said her editor is aware of what happened, adding, "It still makes me think twice before I pitch an article that talks about minorities. That shouldn't happen."

Freitas was also attacked online for another pop culture article that she wrote in 2011 while working as a staff reporter at *O Estado de São Paulo*, and in that case, the newspaper diffused the situation by publishing a supportive editorial, and providing her with a car to transport her to and from the office, she said. The attacks subsided.

But publishers do not always respond that way and, as a result, many female journalists who face such attacks feel compelled to self-censor.

A yearlong interactive study conducted under the auspices of the Internet Governance Forum on how to counter abuse online against women and girls found that such abuse and gender-based violence "impede women's right to freedom of expression by creating environments in which they do not feel safe to express themselves." Women and LGBT journalists who are also minorities, or who are foreign to the countries in which they work, may face additional threats or violence.

"Efforts to combat and address online abuse and gender-based violence often emanate from the developed world and also tend to reflect conditions, cultural perceptions and expectations in developed countries," the study by the Best Practices Forum on Online Abuse and Gender-Based Violence Against Women and Girls[2] at the 2015 Internet Governance Forum concluded.

Few statistics have been compiled about the scope of online harassment and threats against women, nor about LGBT journalists, who face many of the same kinds of attacks. But such problems are widespread according to numerous studies, including a joint survey[3] by the International Women's Media Foundation and the International News Safety Institute, as well as the work[4] of the Association for Progressive Communications, and extensive anecdotal evidence, some of which is reported elsewhere in this book.

Non-journalists and law enforcement officials often suggest that journalists facing online threats stay off Twitter and Facebook, but most journalists consider this an impractical and insufficient response. Journalists are public figures who depend on social media both for researching and disseminating the news, as well as for engaging with their audience and building their public profile. Responding to attacks by vacating their social media space can actually amplify the abuse, which may then go unrebutted, and have economic repercussions for the journalist.

Yet reporting abuse via a social media platform often feels futile, as requests for help go unanswered and unacknowledged, say journalists interviewed for this article and who have spoken out on this topic.

Interviews with journalists and increasing controversy over #gamergate indicate that some managers of electronic and social media platforms are aware of the need to do more to empower users to combat online abuse, but there is disagreement over whether the intermediaries should play a more proactive role—and if so, how. Google briefly toyed with a real-name policy and Twitter[5] has said it will make it easier to flag problematic accounts. All of the major platforms have been criti-cized[6] for lack of transparency on reporting and redress, and failure to include perspectives of non-European/North American women.

Journalist Aviva Rutkin proposed[7] five steps for protection against online threats, including saving records of them and reporting the abuse to the authorities. Some national governments have taken action to enable a more effective response. In South Africa, the Protection from Harassment Act, enacted in 2013, requires electronic communica-tions platforms to assist with court orders to protect against harassment and imposes penalties for not providing necessary information.

In the U.S., users can file complaints with the Internet Crime Complaint Center (IC3) but, as in many other countries, one of the few legal avenues available to victims seeking to remove photos or videos circulating online as part of these harassment campaigns is copyright infringement. Using copyright laws to try to get redress is burdensome and can prolong the harmful impact of online attacks by requiring victims to send copies of offending photos to the authorities, extending their circulation and the harm caused to women.

In many parts of the world, including countries that have spe-cial mechanisms to address online abuse, law enforcement officials are rarely prepared to deal with these types of complaints, and can poten-tially perpetuate the harm by requiring that offending content be fur-ther circulated.

"The police had no idea how to deal with these attacks," Freitas, the Brazilian journalist, observed, offering a common refrain among journalists around the world.

"One prominent obstacle in getting female reporters to talk about their cases has been shame," wrote Kiran Nazish in a *New York Times* column[8] about threats to female journalists in Pakistan. "Women jour-nalists who speak out about their difficulties are publicly humiliated, harassed by supporters of politicians and the establishment. Their fami-lies and colleagues often suffer along with them."

Others have expressed similar sentiments—that the choice of whether to go public is a key issue facing female journalists, since such publicity is a double-edged sword. On one hand, doing so may create a feeling of safety and camaraderie. On the other, it can bring down even greater online wrath and escalate into violence, as has been the case with the #gamergate controversy in the U.S., which has caught female journalists covering video games in the crosshairs of violent online gamers who have sought to destroy their careers and pursue them offline. #Gamergate was a harassment campaign against women in the gaming industry that included attacks against journalists and commentators covering the threats of rape and death that accompanied the vitriol.

Arzu Geybullayeva, an Azerbaijani journalist working in Turkey, who authored a chapter in this book and was the target of online attacks in 2014, has continued to receive periodic hate messages, but said going public made it easier for her to deal with it on a personal and professional level.

"[A]fter I started documenting, sharing, and shaming these people, it got easier," she said. "I think this is the right way to go, to take screen shots, sharing and tweet about these people. I even at some point had the idea of going to these people's profiles and finding some really nice, sweet kind of picture of these people and pairing it with the ugly messages they sent. I still would like to do it."

The latter was among the ideas raised in a session on gender-based violence online at the Stockholm Internet Forum in 2015. "Abuse doesn't come from monsters, but from regular people," Tanya Lokurt, a 34-year-old citizen journalist and Global Voices editor based in Ukraine, told me. She described one episode in which a Russian LGBT activist used this name-and-shame approach[9] to fight back against death threats she received on social media. "It's a very interesting juxtaposition," she said, because "in general, the Russian Internet isn't afraid to use names, they're not afraid that their names will be linked."

In the article Rutkin wrote[10] about how to combat rape and death threats online, she described how another journalist, Australian Alanah Pearce, who covers gaming, noticed that many of the people posting threats on her Facebook page were kids, so "she started tracking down their mothers' profiles and sending screenshots of the concerning messages. One shocked mom forced her son to send Pearce a handwritten letter of apology," according to Rutkin's reporting.[11]

Another remedy proposed by the Best Practices Forum[12] is to require new users to a social media platform to complete a short training program on acceptable behavior and how to report abuse.

Banning anonymity is not a panacea, according to the Best Practices report highlighting the complexity of potential solutions to reducing online harassment and abuse. "A significant portion of online abuse and gender-based violence tends to happen using anonymous accounts or accounts with pseudonyms and/or false names, making it difficult to identify perpetrators," the report noted. "On the other hand, anonymity is recognised as a valuable tool for women to be able to exercise their rights online."

Some policymakers and platforms have proposed to eliminate anonymity online as a way to address this violence, as well as other ills, like extremism and hate speech, but there is disagreement over whether this is the right response. The Brazilian constitution prohibits anonymity, yet that did little to mitigate the attacks against Freitas. Ecuador, Iran, Venezuela and Vietnam also require real-name registration for online services, which amounts to a kind of ban on anonymity, according to the United Nations Special Rapporteur on Freedom of Expression,[13] which did not gauge the effectiveness of such measures. Research[14] by CPJ has found[15] that real-name policies can exacerbate online fraud and censorship while limiting free speech.

The Best Practice report noted the complications of using anonymity to combat online abuse, observing that "while anonymity and the protection of privacy may be vital for the exercise of freedom of expression online, including the right of women to access critical information and support services, these rights may also help to enable online abuse and gender-based violence by providing perpetrators with a cloak of invisibility and, thus, perceived impunity."

And it is not always anonymous strangers who harass female journalists online. Some comments come from male colleagues and sources who engage in lengthy threads that exacerbate the attacks. Nazish, a 33-year-old independent journalist from Pakistan who covers the Middle East, experienced this when she wrote the *Times* article.[16]

Nazish had chronicled the range of threats and violence female journalists in Pakistan face, including her own story of intimidation during an investigation on a security-related issue. Following its publication, she faced a barrage of social media hate. "There were hundreds of tweets calling me a traitor for defaming the country," she told me.

While working on her investigation, Nazish said she was told, "if you write this story you will get killed like your friends. The threats were really specific. I had written about journalist threats often and the key words 'like your friends' was being used specifically to intimidate me." The gender dimension was evident, Nazish said, because much of this harassment came from other journalists in Pakistan who told her she should expect this as a woman and that she wanted only to get attention. "They told me 'it's not a big deal for you to get threats, it's part of the job'; some people said 'you are just attention seeking.' And this is the key difference, when women are targeted, they are expected to take the challenge, and given no empathy."

Nazish chose to respond to some comments that clearly came from trolls, but she did so only once or twice and then decided to let it go. "The problem with trolls is there is no formula or method on which is the right way to deal—some people targeted choose to respond and some don't," she said. "I don't know that there's a right or wrong what you should do; it's really relative."

A 2014 Pew research survey[17] of online harassment in the U.S. found that only about 40 percent of journalists who were harassed online chose to respond, and only about half of them confronted the person online, such as by unfriending or blocking them or addressing the comments. Some of the journalists deleted or reported the comments or changed their username or profile.

Some platforms, including Twitter, allow anonymity or pseudo-anonymity. Others, such as Facebook, prohibit or make anonymity more difficult.

Tom Lowenthal, CPJ technologist, noted that there are two distinct types of platforms: those such as Facebook, where each person is presented with a curated selection of material based on user-defined preferences, and those like Twitter and instant messenger services, where information displayed is not determined by the platform or its algorithms. The result is that different platforms require different approaches to dealing with threats and abuse.

Blocking accounts is another tactic some journalists use to deal with trolls. Lokurt, who writes about Russia and Ukraine, said her co-editor also gets trolled, but unlike attacks on her, the attacks aimed at him focus more on his alleged lack of knowledge or on his political position than on his gender.

Another option is to create block lists, an approach that journalist Randi Harper took after she was harassed over a blog post about sexual harassment during #gamergate. She created a tool[18] for Twitter that automated lists of accounts to block so that the offending #gamergate accounts did not show up in the user's feed. Third party add-ons like Block Together do the same thing, though the features are not integrated or as easy to use as they could be.

"I definitely think social media and communication tools should make these sort of features more widely available," Lowenthal said. He added that although communities of women and marginalized people are learning what tools could be effective when someone becomes targeted, there is a trade-off involved in such an approach. "If there is a large pool of people who hate you, but others are interested in swatting or stalking or physically abusive attacks, tools that make you unaware of these threats could put you at greater risk," he said. "If someone posts my home address, that is info I'd want to know immediately."

The artificiality of the online/offline dichotomy for female journalists in the digital age highlights the need for a range of solutions for addressing online harassment and abuse. Ultimately, solutions to combat and reduce violence against women online or off will need to be multifaceted and take into account shifting norms so that such attacks become unacceptable. Social media platforms also have a responsibility to be more responsive and put greater control in the hands of their users. Ultimately, the best course of action for journalists under attack will be a combination of monitoring and potentially responding to the threats and reporting to platforms and/or authorities, depending on their specific situation and location.

■ ■ ■

Courtney C. Radsch is CPJ's advocacy director and author of the upcoming book Cyberactivism and Citizen Journalism in Egypt: Digital Dissidence and Political Change.

10. The Struggle for Candid Interviews

By Erin Banco

A Yazidi refugee from Iraq holds her child shortly after arriving on the Greek island of Lesbos in November 2015. The author found children most likely to give honest answers to reporters.

Source: AP/Muhammed Muheisen

Inside a four-room apartment in Antakya, Turkey, a town on the border with Syria, more than a dozen men sat on mattresses on the floor. It was just past 10 p.m. and the soldiers, all men in the Free Syrian Army, the rebel opposition group in Syria, were busy coordinating their next trip into the country. The sound of metal clinking emanated from a back room where younger recruits were assembling Kalashnikovs and shoulder-fired missiles.

It was my first interview with a military commander, not just in the Syrian civil war, but in any war. I was 22, looked about 15, but felt older. Never before had I interviewed a soldier. At the time, I didn't fully understand war. I didn't have friends who had served and I didn't know anyone personally fighting in Syria. Yet I was there to interview Riad al-Ahmed, a commander of a battalion in the Free Syrian Army, with another young female journalist and a man who was our Syrian fixer.

We were allowed to interview al-Ahmed only at night at the Antakya house that fighters used to take a break from the fighting. Al-Ahmed was one of the most powerful commanders in the spring of 2012. He had defected from the Syrian army, led by President Bashar Assad, in November the year before (he would be killed in 2013).

When we walked into the house in the spring of 2012, I was prepared for the interview to be a bit awkward. The likelihood was that these men would see me as young and foreign and as a woman, with views on gender that were likely very different than my own. I was nervous, and stumbled over my questions.

What I did not expect was to be almost completely ignored, even though I made an effort to introduce myself in Arabic and to strike up a casual conversation, but the men in the room seemed more interested in talking with my male fixer.

What I found most nerve-racking were the questions they posed when they did acknowledge my presence.

"Wow, you are so young," al-Ahmed said. "You girls are the first women I have had interview me." He then asked questions I hear in almost every interview I have with male soldiers: Are you married? Do you have kids? My answer is always the same: Yes and yes. In fact, I am not married and do not have children.

An older female correspondent had advised me to wear a wedding ring at all times and to carry a picture of children in my bag, in case someone asked. Somehow, she told me, doing so "makes soldiers respect you more." It seemed to work. The interview went on without a hitch once I answered all of al-Ahmed's questions to his satisfaction and told him about the fake toddlers I had waiting back home.

Quite simply, throughout the interview, I became acutely aware of the fact that they didn't think I fit in. I was young and I was female—two characteristics that have consistently caused problems for me throughout my career.

From speaking with women my age in the field, whether reporting in Cairo's Tahrir Square, Aleppo, Baghdad or a house in Antakya, there is one feeling that seems to have stuck with us throughout our reporting in the Middle East: Our gender is often seen by those around us, including many of our male sources, in the same way as our youth and inexperience.

I got my first taste of this in my interview with al-Ahmed. I learned later that there were certain details in that interview that al-Ahmed would hold back, that he would twist.

The interview with al-Ahmed lasted for nearly three hours. I asked all the questions I had written down in my notebook and he gave me information I thought, at the time, was secret and valuable. I came to find out years later, after he died, that al-Ahmed exaggerated certain details. He was not who he said he was. When I returned to report on his death, I learned that he had lied to me and told a male colleague, just a few years older than me, the truth.

I never understood why many of the male soldiers I met in the Middle East tended to exaggerate their status, their role in their battalions, and the events that surrounded certain battles. Maybe they thought I would never find out the truth. Maybe they were trying to impress me. Or maybe they just wanted to get noticed in the press. Whatever the case, it has happened consistently during the past five years.

There's an assumption, one of the men who fought under al-Ahmed's direction told me, that if I did not spend time embedded with them on the front lines, like many of our male colleagues had, I would not know the truth from a lie. Implicit in his comment was that I would have to do what the male reporters had done to earn their respect.

And so, I began embedding with rebels in Syria and Iraq, where I did earn the respect of my military sources—a process many of my male colleagues never had to go through. My male counterparts could sit down for an interview in the same house in Antakya and automatically earn the respect and the truth in one sitting.

Once I reached the frontlines, I experienced an entirely different tone from my interview subjects. There, male fighters constantly told me: "Good for you for being out here" or "Now you probably understand better."

On the flip side, my male colleagues could not as easily speak with female sources, especially in precarious living situations, such as refugee camps, war zones or training camps. As a woman, I am able to gain access to the women and girls, who are often asked to sit in a side room while I interview their father, brother or uncle. As a woman, I can sit with a mother and her children alone without her husband and speak to her candidly. I can ask her about her daily life and how she gets by day to day. Women often feel comfortable sitting with me and talking about their mental state and struggles with post-traumatic stress disorder. They tell me tales of sleepless nights and wetting the bed every time a plane flies by. They find comfort in speaking with female journalists because of the divide between men and women in their own culture. That comfort provides me with access to stories about the broader implications of conflict than are available to journalists who are limited to interviewing soldiers.

At a makeshift refugee camp on the border of Syria and Turkey, I sat with a woman and her three children in a tent. The woman, Fatima, had been living in the camp for nearly a year. Her husband was in Aleppo, fighting the Islamic State group. She was alone in the camp with no money and no reliable way to get food for her children.

Despite our ability to talk openly about her sexual abuse in the camp and her husband's absence, she too asked me up front: Are you married? Do you have children?

Fatima asked me this question the same day I found out the truth about al-Ahmed. When she asked, I smiled, surprised that a woman was asking me the same question I had pegged to male soldiers. This time, though, I told the truth. Maybe I was acknowledging the gender divisions I had experienced while interviewing in the Middle East— trusting a woman and writing off al-Ahmed.

After years of traveling and interviewing men and women across the Middle East, I came to realize that those two answers did not hold as much weight as I had thought. Al-Ahmed still lied, which pushed me to go to the frontlines and see things for myself. And with Fatima, the truth, my truth, made her more comfortable opening up to me.

In September 2015, I reported for two weeks from Munich and Budapest, where I interviewed unaccompanied minors—children who had made their way to Europe from places like Syria and Iraq, alone.

In Munich, I met a boy named Ali. He was 15 and traveled from Syria to Europe. He had been smuggled into Germany and hoped to eventually find a way to get his parents to join him in Europe. He told me harrowing stories of stolen passports and trafficking—all tales that could have put him in danger. After just two days, he trusted me enough to tell his story to the world. I verified Ali's story with German authorities and his friends who traveled with him. Everything he told me was spot on, nothing embellished.

I have found that the only people I interview in the Middle East during wartime who consistently tell the truth, and disregard my gender, are children. Although gaining access to interview them can be difficult, children are typically honest, even when lying might benefit them.

■ ■ ■

Erin Banco is a Middle East reporter for International Business Times *and holds a master's of public administration from Columbia's School of International and Public Affairs.*

11. Heroines for Press Freedom

By María Salazar-Ferro

Diane Foley, left, mother of James Foley, the photojournalist killed by Islamic State militants in 2014, and Debra Tice, mother of freelance journalist Austin Tice, who has been missing since he was taken captive in Syria in 2012, take part in a forum at the Newseum in Washington on February 4, 2015.

Source: AP/Molly Riley

L ate on the evening of September 16, 2000, 31-year-old Ukrainian investigative journalist Georgy Gongadze left a colleague's house in Kiev and headed home, where his wife and young daughters awaited him. He never made it.

"Those first couple of days were really blurry," his wife, Myroslava Gongadze, recently recalled. "I was in a sort of limbo and didn't know what to do." Days after her husband's disappearance, local officials ruled out a political motive despite his sharp criticism of the Ukrainian government. In mid-November, a burned, headless body was identified as the journalist's, and within weeks, an opposition leader leaked taped recordings of what appeared to be conversations between then-president Leonid Kuchma and other high-ranking officials on possible ways of "dealing" with Gongadze. So Myroslava Gongadze, a lawyer by training, decided to step in. If she, who was so personally affected by the murder, did not take the lead, she said, no one else was going to fight for the truth.

Using her legal knowledge, a network of media contacts and a steadfast drive, Gongadze worked with a group of local and international journalists and human rights organizations to build a legal case and a public campaign. Fifteen years on, four former officials have been convicted of murder while the European Court of Human Rights has ruled that the Ukrainian government is liable for the journalist's death. Despite her success, Gongadze says that there have been times when she has been ready to quit. "I have wanted to change my name, to disappear, to change my life, to become a different person. And then I realize that this is it. This is me."

Since I began working for the Committee to Protect Journalists in 2005, I have met and worked with a number of other women from around the world who, like Myroslava Gongadze, have become prominent figures in press freedom campaigns. They are the mothers, wives, daughters, sisters, girlfriends and colleagues of journalists who go missing, are held hostage, injured or imprisoned, or who have been killed. Though they have male counterparts, a majority of the impromptu campaigners that I have encountered are women. They come from different countries and backgrounds, while their individual battles are strongly rooted in personal stories. Yet they share an unrelenting commitment to truth and justice that transcends those particular experiences.

Is gender the root of their commitment? The frequency of cases such as Gongadze's would seem to point in that direction. But in speaking with her and others who have waged similar fights, gender seems not to play a predictable role. The women recognize a pattern, but they also raise contradictions in their analysis of what has driven them to the forefront of campaigns in some of the world's most visible attacks on journalists.

In November 2015, I interviewed four women whose lives were fundamentally transformed by a single devastating event that, within days—hours in one case—had turned them from wife, mother or friend into a kind of combatant. My goal in interviewing them was to dissect battlefield stories and strategies in order to understand the role that gender had played. I spoke with Gongadze; with Sandhya Eknelygoda, wife of missing Sri Lankan political cartoonist Prageeth Eknelygoda; with Diane Foley, mother of American freelancer James Foley, who was taken hostage and brutally murdered in Syria; and with Soleyana S. Gebremichael, a founding member of the Ethiopian Zone 9 bloggers collective, several of whose colleagues spent more than a year in jail.

Of the four, only Eknelygoda told me that gender was key to her struggle. The other narratives were less clear-cut. Foley and Soleyana (who, like many Ethiopians, goes only by her first name) both said gender does not drive the kind of battle they have waged. Temperament and commitment do. In fact, Foley said, her son "is the hero. Jim is the one who keeps me going," adding that she developed a passion for justice from him.

For Gongadze, it is not the fighters' gender that is at play, but rather the gender of those on whose behalf they are fighting. "I guess it's mostly the men who are journalists who get into danger," she said. The numbers CPJ collects on journalist murders support that assertion: Of the 1,175 journalists killed since CPJ began tracking these cases in 1992, 93 percent were male. "Then who is left to fight for them?" Gongadze asked, answering almost immediately: "Their women."

When Prageeth Eknelygoda, a fierce critic of the government of former Sri Lankan president Mahinda Rajapaksa, failed to come home on January 24, 2010, a few days before the country's presidential election, Sandhya Eknelygoda rushed to the local police station to report him missing. Officers laughed at her, saying he was probably with another woman or had staged his own disappearance, Eknelygoda said, but she persevered. Later that month, she met with the senior superintendent of police, and when he, too, dismissed her concerns, she filed a complaint with the Human Rights Commission of Sri Lanka. Faced with silence, Eknelygoda began to write letters to high-ranking officials. When those went unanswered, she filed a habeas corpus asking for Prageeth's whereabouts or for his body. And when this effort also failed, Eknelygoda reached out to the international community and began a series of public appearances around the world to highlight her husband's case.

In January 2015, Sri Lanka held early presidential elections and the opposition candidate, Maithripala Sirisena, surprisingly defeated Rajapaksa, who was seeking a third term. By this time, Eknelygoda's quest had blown up into a global mission for truth not only for her husband and other journalists but also for thousands of disappeared Sri Lankans for whom she has become a de facto spokeswoman. Almost immediately after being elected, Sirisena pledged to reopen the files of missing and killed journalists, and by the time I spoke with Eknelygoda in 2015, five army officers and two civilians had been arrested in connection to Prageeth Eknelygoda's disappearance.

Armed men kidnapped Jim Foley, an American freelance journalist, in Syria on Thanksgiving Day as he was making his way to Turkey. His whereabouts were unknown until August 19, 2014, when the militant Islamic State group posted a video online showing the journalist's brutal beheading as a warning and reprisal toward the government of U.S. president Barack Obama. At the request of Foley's parents, Diane and John Foley, his disappearance had not been made public until January 2013, when they launched a vocal campaign seeking his release. Almost immediately, Diane Foley became a voice for the families of other American hostages.

After her son's brutal killing, a devastated Foley decided that she would not give up her fight. "I could not let someone so extraordinary die," Foley told me over the phone on her way home from Washington, D.C., after having testified before the U.S. Congress. Within three weeks of her son's murder, she had filed the necessary paperwork to start the James W. Foley Legacy Foundation, which champions causes that her son was passionate about: support for American hostages, greater rights for freelance journalists and better education for under-privileged youth.

So far, Foley and her foundation have had a hand in important changes to two of these three issues. In February 2015, a coalition of news executives, press freedom groups and individual journalists, including CPJ, agreed to a set of global principles for freelancers' safety. To date, the principles have been signed by 78 organizations. Four months later, the Obama administration announced changes to U.S. hostage policy. According to news reports, the change in policy will allow government officials to communicate and negotiate with groups holding hostages and help American families seeking to do the same, while an interagency hostage recovery "fusion cell" will coordinate efforts to free American captives. Though encouraged by the progress, Foley says she will believe there has been real change only when an American hostage has come home.

■ ■ ■

Ethiopian authorities in Addis Ababa rounded up six young bloggers who were part of an independent collective know as Zone 9. On that day, Soleyana, one of the group's founding members, was traveling out-side the country. From Nairobi, Kenya, Soleyana stayed informed of the day's events in real time through her friend and colleague Zelalem Kibret, until he, too, was detained. That evening, having reached each of her friends' families by phone, Soleyana worked with Zone 9 co-founder Endalk Chala, who was also abroad, on a press release calling for the government to release their colleagues from prison, she told me from her new home in Maryland. She said they subse-quently launched a formidable social media campaign with the hashtag #FreeZone9Bloggers.

In July 2015, more than a year after the Zone 9 arrests and weeks before President Obama visited Ethiopia, Ethiopian authorities released two of the bloggers. Three months later, the rest were freed. In November, CPJ awarded Zone 9 with an International Press Freedom Award.

Soleyana and the other women I interviewed had a clear goal from the beginning, but their campaign strategies, they told me, have been built ad hoc. The week after her husband's disappearance, with no action or clear answers from local authorities, friends convinced a disoriented Myroslava Gongadze to hold a press conference. Accompanied by her four-year-old twins, Gongadze told journalists that her husband hadn't come home. She then voiced a call to action. "I said that they needed to support me; that the journalistic community needed to support me. I said it's him today, you tomorrow," she said. "But there was no real strategy until I realized that there was not going to be justice in Ukraine. Then, I had a strategy and I called for a special investigation with support from [the International Federation of Journalists, Reporters Without Borders] and CPJ. We did reports on the progress of the investigation. And we analyzed all the possibilities for international justice." Gongadze eventually filed a suit with the Strasbourg, France-based European Court of Human Rights, claiming the government had failed to protect her husband and to properly investigate his murder. In 2005, the court found the Ukrainian government liable for Georgy Gongadze's death and awarded his wife 100,000 euros, about $118,000 at the time, in damages.

Media attention, whether intentional or impromptu, good or bad, has also played a pivotal role in these campaigns. Charismatic in their own way, each woman has found and fostered an intricate relationship with the media. For Gongadze and Eknelygoda, their husbands' colleagues have been crucial. Local journalists, they told me, have been among their closest allies, while local and international media have not only helped broadcast their calls for justice but also continuously highlighted their work.

"There are many sympathizers to my work in the media, and of course there are others who are not cooperative," Eknelygoda told me via Skype from her Colombo, Sri Lanka, kitchen, with her teenage son acting as our translator. "But I have many friends in the media who understand me and give publicity to Prageeth's case. There is a lot of support for me as a person and for the cause that I am fighting. There is also comfort and satisfaction in the fact that the media continue to be sympathetic. It is so important to give the case exposure in the media."

Soleyana's case is a little different from the others in its approach to the media. For most of the 18 months that her six friends spent in prison, Soleyana worked with two other bloggers—Endalk, who lives in the U.S., and Jomanex Kasaye, who managed to escape Ethiopia and has since settled in Sweden—publicizing the case mostly on social media. "Our strategy was to highlight the journalists as human beings: family members, friends, etc.—not as politicians," she said. "We wanted to show their human side, and we used social media to tell their stories so that other young people in the country could relate to them." The end goal of their social media campaign, Soleyana said, was to keep the international community and the Ethiopian public informed and engaged in their calls for the bloggers' release.

Though Soleyana said responsibility for the campaign, like the blog that led to the imprisonments, was shared with Endalk and Jomanex, Endalk said Soleyana's charisma helped make a strong yet likeable public case for the release of their colleagues. "She is happy to engage anyone online or offline," Endalk said. As part of her strategy, Soleyana also highlighted the Zone 9 case at meetings with international groups and high-ranking officials, including Obama and U.S. Secretary of State John Kerry.

In Endalk's view, Soleyana was the force that kept the group going. "Gender is very important and I think it is directly related to her role in the blog and the campaign," he told me. "Before we even started, before the arrests, Soli was very good at organizing stuff and she had a very important leadership role in putting the group together. She is so demanding and her standards are so high, she is always asking us to produce things. Even when we remind her that this is voluntary work, she keeps pushing. And this role continued after the arrests."

Despite growing external strategic support, which Gongadze, Eknelygoda and Soleyana credit as necessary to their success, their campaigns could not have survived the long haul without what is best described as a kind of religious devotion on their part. When I asked Gongadze how she referred to the work that she had been doing, she said, "Finding justice for Georgy was just my life. I had no name for it."

All four women said they were driven by devotion, passion and strong personal feelings—concepts that are hard to define, as Gongadze told me. The role of gender is likewise difficult to gauge. Foley noted that women can be very passionate, "but so can men." Eknelygoda insisted that "women feel a different way about relationships than men do. There is a clear difference in the way in which men and women even think about these situations. Men tend to give up after some time, but women continue to fight."

The fight itself, regardless of what drove it, has exacted a toll on all of them. Eknelygoda and Soleyana quit their jobs almost immediately to devote all their time to the campaigns. In both cases, this decision meant having to rely heavily upon external financial support. Soleyana said she had to apply to international organizations for emergency grants, which she administered, to pay for campaign costs and basic needs for the families of those who were imprisoned. Eknelygoda received similar support, but financing her years-long campaign while supporting her family, she told me, echoing Gongadze, has made a difficult road to justice even harder.

Some of her greatest difficulties have been financial, Eknelygoda said. During a 2012 interview, a clearly pained Eknelygoda had told me that fearful friends and family had abandoned her and her two sons after her husband's disappearance. Having quit her part-time clerical job and lost her husband's income, she was forced to turn to donations from concerned individuals and to emergency support from international organizations, including several grants from CPJ's Journalist Assistance Program. In 2015, as the legal case continued to require most of her time, Eknelygoda said she was paying her bills through the proceeds from a small catering business that provides what she calls "rice packages" at small events, allowing her to continue devoting most of her time to her activism.

There have been other bumps on the road, she said. Perhaps the roughest, which have shaken her to the point of questioning her devotion, have come at the hands of local authorities, who until recently ignored and disregarded her systematically while countering her campaign with unsubstantiated claims. In 2012, then-Attorney General Mohan Peiri told United Nations officials that Prageeth Eknelygoda was hiding in a foreign country and that the campaign to solve his disappearance was a hoax. Six years on, the pain associated with financial, political and social isolation remains raw for Eknelygoda.

Stories like Eknelygoda's—of degradation at the hands of local authorities—are not uncommon. In my 10 years of reporting on press freedom violations, I have repeatedly been told of similar disregard for family members, many of them women, who are seeking support or information about a loved one. This group includes Gongadze, who, recalling the day she reported her husband missing, said local police officers "were just laughing at me, telling me to go away." With a knowing smile, she said officials told her that her husband probably left her for another woman.

Part of Diane and John Foley's decision not to make their son's disappearance public until January 2013 was based, Diane Foley has frequently said, on encouragement from the Obama administration to remain quiet in order to protect her son. "I trusted much too long and we failed. We were duped," Foley said. According to her, authorities failed to conduct a proper and timely investigation into her son's kidnapping; gave her and her husband little or misleading information about their son's situation; and refused to negotiate with her son's captors while warning her and her husband that they could face prosecution if they paid the ransom. "Though I do not blame anyone," she said, "we did let policy get in the way of helping."

Despite her disclaimer, Foley feels that the government failed her son, and that so did the media and organizations dedicated to protecting journalists, including CPJ. She believes that despite the initial media blackout, people active in the field could have more actively supported her quest. "Jim had vanished and a lot of journalists knew war zones and knew Syria. They could have helped because they knew more than the government, but they didn't call us. They never come forward with information," she said. As Foley explained her attempts at accountability, it was apparent that she felt a deep sense of isolation rooted in her campaign—not dissimilar to the feeling Eknelygoda also described.

Beyond personal hardships, these women shared other considerable obstacles. Most notably, they have all faced direct threats. Since going public with her quest for her husband's whereabouts, on several occasions Eknelygoda has received phone threats from unidentified individuals who accuse her of being a traitor. Foley said she has been harassed on social media by people who consider her open criticism of the U.S. government an attack on the American way of life. Both have been shaken, but neither has considered the threats serious. The threats against Gongadze and Soleyana, on the other hand, forced them into exile.

"Right away I started to receive threats," Gongadze said. In the months after her husband was killed, Gongadze became aware that her every move was being tracked, she told me, adding that he too had been trailed.

Colleagues with connections to Ukraine's security apparatus, Gongadze said, told her that her phones had been tapped and warned her not to discuss anything important. "So, at that point, I sent my girls to live with my parents," she said. "I asked a friend to take them, and nobody knew where they were. They had taken my husband and I did not want my kids at risk because I had decided to go public."

Then, Gongadze said, a local politician handed her an alleged recording of President Kuchma telling his chief of staff to do something to stop her and the editor of *Ukrainska Pravda*, her husband's outlet. In the recording, the man purported to be Kuchma urged the other official to stop Gongadze's activities, which he said had become a nuisance, she told me. Though Gongadze says she did not know how the recordings were made, she began to seriously fear for her life and that of her children. A member of the opposition had earlier leaked another set of secretly recorded tapes in which Kuchma, who served as president of Ukraine from 1994 to 2005, is overheard plotting with other high-ranking officials, including his chief of staff, on different ways to get rid of Georgy Gongadze. Kuchma was indicted in 2011 on abuse-of-office charges related to the Gongadze case, though he rejected accusations that he had a role in the journalist's murder. However, according to press reports, he did not deny that the voice in the first set of tapes was his, though he claimed the recordings had been doctored.

Gongadze and her daughters left Ukraine for the United States, where they were granted political asylum in 2001.

Soleyana also traveled to the U.S., leaving East Africa a month after the April 2014 Zone 9 arrests. Until then, she had remained in Nairobi, Kenya, where hundreds of other exiled Ethiopians, including dozens of journalists, live. Fearing the long arm of the Ethiopian government, Soleyana and Jomanex, who had fled on the night of the arrests, decided to leave East Africa.

Soon after Soleyana left the region, her mother's Addis Ababa home was raided in what she described as a fruitless effort by Ethiopian authorities to find solid evidence linking Zone 9 to terrorist organizations. Despite a lack of evidence, in July 2014, an Ethiopian court charged Soleyana with terrorism in absentia. She was acquitted, also in absentia, a year later. "At that point," she said, "it became clear that I was not going to go home."

Self-imposed exile has given Gongadze and Soleyana the security and space to continue their work. Leaving Sri Lanka for short periods of time and speaking publicly at the international level has also given weight to Eknelygoda's campaign and, in a way, afforded her protection. Eknelygoda is now an award-winning international figure who can open doors that six years ago would likely have been slammed shut.

The quest for justice has become so entwined with all the women's lives and identities that even after some form of resolution, they continue to define themselves through their quest. In all four cases a commitment that began as personal has developed into a mission for justice and greater change.

Despite the shift in the campaign, and in the way that she is perceived, Eknelygoda sees her new goal and role as an extension of the mission she set out on the day her husband did not come home. "When I was fighting individually [for Prageeth], what I determined first was to not let the case of a disappearance be disappeared," she said. "Now I work to represent the voices of the voiceless using my voice. Those are the reasons that I am where I am now."

Asked about her husband's possible fate, Eknelygoda said she fears she will never know the truth, but that she finds solace in knowing that her continued advocacy will in some way keep him alive. "Whatever they say, whatever the truth is, he is alive for me, he is alive in my fight," she said.

■ ■ ■

María Salazar-Ferro is CPJ's Journalist Assistance Program coordinator. She covered the Americas region for CPJ for four years and has written reports on exiled and missing journalists and impunity in journalist murders. She has represented CPJ on missions around the globe.

12. Fighting Words

By Kerry Paterson

A judge sits at a hearing in the International Criminal Court in The Hague in March 2014. In conflict zones, it is not unusual for police, local militias, national armies, or foreign peacekeepers to be implicated in sexual assaults.

Source: AP/Phil Nijhuis

"When I cried, he slapped me hard and put his hand over my mouth." That is how a 12-year-old girl in the Central African Republic described an episode in which a man found her hiding in the bathroom of her home in the wee hours of August 2, 2015, dragged her outside, and raped her, hidden from view behind a truck.

The man was allegedly wearing the blue helmet and vest of the United Nations peacekeeping forces, and a medical examination of the girl found evidence consistent with sexual assault, according to an Amnesty International report.

The New York Times and the *Guardian* later reported that the alleged rapist was one of 17 U.N. personnel facing accusations of sexual abuse since the mission began operations in Bangui, the capital of the Central African Republic (CAR), in April 2014.

The allegations against the U.N. peacekeepers in the CAR came as the U.N. mission there was already tasked with investigating accusations that French peacekeepers had forced a group of young homeless boys to perform sex acts on them in exchange for money or food. In April 2015, the U.N.'s failure to address these allegations of rape and sexual violence against children in Bangui at the hands of French peacekeepers was highlighted in a document leaked to the *Guardian* titled "Sexual Abuse on Children by International Armed Forces."[1] A senior U.N. staffer, Anders Kompass, was suspended for submitting the report to French authorities who visited Bangui. The suspension was later ruled unlawful and lifted.

The leaked document makes clear that the U.N. not only was aware of the ongoing abuses but also made no attempt to protect the children, while striving to cover their own inaction. *Guardian* journalist Sandra Laville reported, "The U.N. has faced several scandals in the past relating to its failure to act over paedophile rings operating in the Democratic Republic of Congo, Kosovo and Bosnia."

Prosecutions of wartime sexual violence are rare, but when they do occur, it is usually a direct result of documentation of the assaults. The historic lack of documentation and acknowledgment concerning gender-related and sexual crimes, as well as the significant impact that meaningful documentation can have in ensuring that the crimes are addressed, is highlighted in two published papers, "Prosecuting Wartime

Rape and Other Gender-Related Crimes Under International Law: Extraordinary Advances, Enduring Obstacles" by legal scholar Kelly Askin,[2] and "Rape as a Crime of War: A Medical Perspective" by scholars Shana Swiss and Joan E. Giller.[3]

Advocates of investigating and prosecuting such cases say journalists are integral to the process because they collect data, share testimony, shed light on reported incidents, and give voice to victims who might otherwise be silent, as happened in the case of the young boys and the French peacekeepers and that of the girl raped in Bangui.

In conflict zones, it is not unusual for police, local militias, national armies or foreign peacekeepers to be implicated in rapes and sexual assaults. Journalists with the freedom to report the stories are often seen as the best hope that justice will be served, according to data collected by the Women Under Siege project, which investigates the use of rape and sexualized violence as a weapon of war. When the media's freedom to report such stories is undermined, or when censorship prohibits the sharing of information, it has the effect of perpetuating impunity in such crimes, potentially leading to further violence, and sometimes compounds trauma for victims, who are once again silenced.

In response to publicity over the alleged involvement of peacekeepers in rape and sexualized violence against civilians, including children, U.N. secretary-general Ban Ki-moon announced on August 12, 2015, that the head of the U.N.'s CAR mission, Babacar Gaye, had resigned his post; news reports[4] said he was fired. In addition to incidences of sexualized violence at the hands of peacekeepers in the CAR, including the rape of the girl and a similar episode in eastern CAR, the media reported on what many saw as an inadequate response to the abuses by the French peacekeepers.

"None of this gets the light of day until a journalist gets wind of it," Paula Donovan, co-founder and co-director of AIDS-Free World, said of the media's role in Gaye's firing. According to Donovan, who has worked with UNICEF and as senior adviser to the U.N. special envoy for HIV/AIDS in Africa, "Using the media is actually the only way to get the facts on the record … When the public gets incensed, and they only do that when the press is involved, only then do member states respond."

At a December 9, 2015, hearing in Washington on the U.N.'s peacekeeping missions, U.S. ambassador to the U.N. Samantha Power testified[5] that although improvements have been made in the reporting of and response to such allegations, "Too often we hear from NGOs or from journalists about sexual abuse and exploitation, rather ... than from the U.N. itself." Power said the U.N. needs to improve its ability to investigate allegations of peacekeeper abuse to reduce the time "between an allegation and an actual follow-through."

On December 22, 2015, *The New York Times* reported[6] that the U.N.'s high commissioner for human rights, Zeid Ra'ad al-Hussein, said he had ordered subordinates to inform him immediately when allegations of such abuse first arise, even when doing so meant jumping the customary chain of command. Hussein said he did "not want to be in a situation where I read somewhere in the press, or I hear from another part of the U.N., that a human rights officer has begun to look into an allegation and I don't know about it."

The Central African Republic is not unique when it comes to failure by authorities to address sexual abuse. In the Democratic Republic of Congo (DRC), where about 48 women are raped per hour, according to a study published in the American Journal of Public Health in June 2011, the government has a long history of failing to meaningfully respond to sexualized violence against its population.

Karen Naimer, director of the Program on Sexual Violence in Conflict at Physicians for Human Rights (PHR), a New York–based nonprofit that uses science and medicine to document and call attention to mass atrocities and severe human rights violations, has pushed for prosecutions of crimes of sexual violence in East and Central Africa. She said she has seen firsthand the role that the media—both domestic and international—can play in turning the tide in cases of systemic rape.

In 2013, in the small eastern DRC town of Kavumu, PHR staff began hearing stories about dozens of children who had been abducted from their homes at night, sexually assaulted and then returned home. Though the perpetrators of the crimes have still not been identified, pressure to investigate came primarily from media platforms, such as Reuters, *Foreign Policy* and the BBC. The international media can often report more freely on episodes of sexual violence in countries where press freedom is limited. But the local and national press can also profoundly influence local approaches to and understandings of these crimes.

"We have really struggled from the outset—we at Physicians for Human Rights, and other organizations on the ground—to push for meaningful investigations and prosecutions for these cases," Naimer said of the Kavumu abductions. She said the government in Kinshasa did little until international media reported the story, which hadn't been reported by local news outlets. She said many grassroots groups and local community members were trying to get attention to the problem from local officials and political leaders in Kinshasa with limited success, until PHR shared information about the cases with journalist Lauren Wolfe, a columnist at *Foreign Policy* who is director of the Women Under Siege project and a former senior editor at the Committee to Protect Journalists. "By printing the story and the challenges to pursuing these cases in any meaningful way, and publishing it in *Foreign Policy*,[7] it had a huge impact, and then of course the BBC picked it up and others have followed, and that really put a lot of pressure on the government, both in the capital and in the east, to respond," Naimer said. Both victims and officials were encouraged to come forward and ask questions about what was being done, she said.

Still, Naimer said local media can have a profound and often more immediate impact for survivors of sexual violence, given their proximity and ability to relate to the stories being told.

"One of the huge challenges is the stigma associated with sexualized violence, and journalists and the media have a huge role to play to roll back that stigma, to put the stigma on the perpetrators and to empower survivors, and give their experience more acknowledgment and respect," Naimer said. "Not only is there a role that journalists have to expose the problem, but they can also reshape the discourse."

Local journalists who do so face their own risks, Wolfe said. "The few journalists who've dared to report on sexualized violence in Congo in many cases have received threats," Wolfe said. "It's not a place where it's easy to talk about such things. Victims have a hard time speaking about it and even journalists are given the message that it's not something you should be reporting on."

Local journalists face censorship, self-censorship and imprisonment in many countries, with Eritrea, Somalia and Ethiopia among the worst offenders, according to CPJ research. In 2011, a group of journalists was criminally charged[8] in Sudan for reporting on the rape and torture of a young activist, and in 2013, a journalist was arrested[9] in Somalia after interviewing an alleged rape victim. In 2015, a Nigerian journalist was threatened[10] after he reported on the alleged rape of boys at a school in the northern city of Kano. In such countries, international media can be crucial.

Veteran journalist Mae Azango received the message to which Wolfe alluded when she set out to report on sensitive gender-related topics in her West African country, Liberia. Azango, a recipient of a CPJ International Press Freedom Award[11] in 2012, received threats[12] and was eventually forced into hiding with her nine-year-old daughter for her reporting on the widespread practice of female genital mutilation in the country.

Discussing her ordeal in 2012, Azango described the unique challenges of being a female journalist attempting to tackle a taboo story. Yet she continued reporting on a topic that had concerned her for years—the struggles of Liberian women and girls. The power of Azango's voice—as a woman, as a mother, and as a local reporting on her own country—became clear when Liberian officials took an unprecedented step of ordering the suspension[13] of female genital mutilation throughout the country.

"I am a passionate person and I can transform my passion into something that will help others," Azango said.

"Unfortunately, local journalists have to be the martyrs and the heroes in this," Donovan said. International journalists are often better positioned to bring about responses from multilateral bodies because, she said, "The U.N. is not afraid of local press. They are afraid that international media will pick up a local story." In Donovan's view, "Good journalists don't simply unearth scandals or expose hypocrisy. Sad to say, the media have become the conscience of the U.N., the missing half of the checks-and-balances equation."

A U.N. spokeswoman acknowledged that journalists are important to ensuring transparency and accountability when it comes to unearthing abuses, but disagreed that the organization does not adequately respond except when cases are highly publicized.

"The media has a critical role to play in reporting sexual exploitation and abuse," said Ismini Palla, the acting deputy chief of public affairs for the U.N. Departments of Peacekeeping Operations and Field Support. "Media reporting in a responsible and fair manner has always been supported by U.N. Peacekeeping, and it is in line with the core principles of the organization." Palla noted that the U.N. provides regular and comprehensive updates to the media regarding cases of sexualized abuse, and said it is not true that the organization investigates only when the media is involved. "Sexual exploitation and abuse by U.N. personnel is unacceptable," she said. "Every case is investigated and we are committed to zero complacency and zero impunity."

According to Palla, "U.N. Peacekeeping has been transparent about the issue through regular public reports, special press briefings as well as online data available on the Department of Field Support's Conduct and Discipline website which are being updated on a monthly basis. The secretary-general publishes an annual report on special measures for protection from sexual exploitation and abuse as well as supplementary data with the status updates of every allegation."

Palla said the U.N. is also reviewing proposals, including for response teams, complaint systems, punitive measures and the establishment of a trust fund for victims' assistance. "Consultations are also ongoing with the General Assembly to begin providing country-specific information on credible allegations that are being investigated," she said.

Yet even when such stories are reported, censorship is sometimes used to silence the voices of survivors of sexualized violence. In September 2015, the government of the DRC initially banned[14] the screening or circulation of a documentary film, "The Man Who Mends Women: The Wrath of Hippocrates," which tells the story of Bukavu's Panzi Hospital and gynecologist Denis Mukwege, who treats rape victims in the war-torn eastern region of the country. The film was banned on the grounds that it reflected poorly on the country's military and that testimony was mistaken or false, according to a press statement from the minister of information, Lambert Mende. Naimer said that when a documentary is dismissed by a government because it reveals an uncomfortable truth, "It sends a very chilling message to the people." Censorship, though not always effective, "can be very retraumatizing," she said.

"Many women in the Congo wanted to tell their stories—they wanted to be heard," Naimer said.

On October 19, 2015, after more than a month of international coverage by outlets including the *Guardian*, Al Jazeera, Reuters and *Foreign Policy*, the government of the DRC allowed the film to be broadcast on national television. In Wolfe's view, the international media has a special responsibility to see that the stories of victims of sexual violence are heard. Local media may not always be able to tell those stories, she said, adding, "But if you show up and there are people who want their stories heard, and you can tell them, I think you have a responsibility to."

■ ■ ■

Kerry Paterson is the research associate for CPJ's Africa program. She was an associate editor of the Journal for International Law and International Relations*, and has worked with Médecins Sans Frontières, the Women's Media Center's Women Under Siege Project and Massachusetts General Hospital's Division of Global Health and Human Rights.*

13. Harassed and Jailed

By Arzu Geybullayeva

The author, like imprisoned journalist Khadija Ismayilova, has been subject to an ugly campaign to discredit her in the eyes of the Azerbaijani people.

Source: Anna Zamejc

I t feels strange to be writing about friends in jail. You wonder what kind of a friend you are—free to breathe the air, to walk the streets, to continue to work, while your friends cannot. Why do you deserve this privilege?

But such is the state of freedom in Azerbaijan, where innocent men and women—especially journalists and human rights activists—are thrown into jail on trumped-up charges, for lengthy periods, because they attempted to report the truth. None of my friends in jail—and sadly, I have a few—are criminals. They are brave people who spoke the truth and confronted the government. They worked tirelessly to make Azerbaijan a better place.

One of them is Khadija Ismayilova[1] (sometimes written Ismayil), a well-known investigative journalist who also hosted a daily radio show called "After Work" on Radio Azadliq, the Azeri service of the U.S. government-funded Radio Free Europe/Radio Liberty, which was among several international organizations shut down by the government in 2014. For a brief time, she was also the station's bureau chief in Baku, and for three years she was a key member of the Organized Crime and Corruption Reporting Project, which exposed fraud by the family of Azerbaijani president Ilham Aliyev and other government officials.

Aliyev was elected president in 2003, succeeding his father, former KGB general Heydar Aliyev. The transition was swift and seamless in a country with a poor record of free and fair elections. In what many international observers described[2] as a flawed election, Ilham Aliyev won an absolute majority with 75.3 percent of the vote. In 2009, after two terms in power, the younger Aliyev managed to scrap presidential term limits through a national referendum and in 2013 was elected to a third term with 84 percent of the vote.

Starting in 2010, Khadija Ismayilova detailed corruption in the highest echelons of Azerbaijan's ruling establishment, especially among the Aliyevs, from lucrative business deals awarded to companies connected to the president's family to the workings of offshore companies and properties owned by family members, including the president's teenaged son, Heydar Aliyev, who was named after his grandfather.

In her first[3] big investigative piece, Ismayilova reported on the Aliyevs' connections to AZAL, or Azerbaijan Airlines, which had bypassed the government's State Committee on Privatization of State Property to privatize its service branches. She also reported that the ruling family was personally benefiting from the construction[4] of the Crystal Hall concert venue, built to host the Eurovision Song Contest in 2012, and had acquired full rights to a lucrative gold field exploration.[5] In 2014, she reported on connections between the Aliyev daughters Arzu and Leyla and the country's largest telephone company, Azercell. Neither the government nor the president and his family have denied these allegations nor otherwise responded to the stories.

The ruling family is known for guarding its privacy, with the exception of appearances at glitzy galas, where journalists asking tough questions are not welcome. Privacy, however, was not a luxury extended to Ismayilova once she had angered powerful people with her investigative reporting. Attempts to silence her included a March 2012 online posting of a sex tape[6] involving her, which she said followed a letter she had received with intimate photographs and the threat: "Whore, behave. Or you will be defamed." Envelopes containing the same photos were also sent to her boyfriend, relatives and opposition media outlets, she said.

The release of a sex tape could be particularly damaging to a woman in a conservative, Muslim-majority country, with all the potential ramifications, including the possibility of an honor killing, according to traditional Azerbaijani customs, said Giorgi Gogia of Human Rights Watch during a ceremony that awarded Ismayilova the organization's Alison Des Forges Award for Extraordinary Activism in 2015.

In Azerbaijan, gender-related attacks are among many mechanisms used in attempts to silence critical media, and they are not limited to women. Men, too, have been the targets of sexual revelations. In many cases, such attacks are precursors to imprisonment. Sometimes, the harassment extends to journalists' relatives, forcing some to leave their jobs or feel compelled to denounce family members for the work they do.

Although other journalists, both male and female, have been harassed, Ismayilova is the first female journalist to be imprisoned. She was first arrested in December 2014 on charges of inciting a man to commit suicide—a charge widely criticized by human rights organizations as bogus,[7] for which she was later cleared. While she was in pretrial custody, she was charged with several alleged crimes,[8] including embezzlement and tax evasion, and on those she was convicted. On September 1, 2015, she was sentenced to seven and a half years in prison.[9]

As this was happening, the government increased its use of ruthless tactics against women and elder journalists and activists, both groups traditionally treated with respect in Azerbaijan. In a span of six months in 2014, while Azerbaijan held the chairmanship of the Committee of Ministers of the Council of Europe, conditions deteriorated for independent media outlets, nongovernmental organizations, youth activist organizations and opposition groups. As more restrictive laws were introduced, some civil society organizations suspended their activities, prominent rights defenders were detained, travel bans were selectively imposed, and many organizations' bank accounts—as well as those of individuals associated with them—were frozen.

In August 2015, two prominent Azerbaijani activists, Leyla Yunus and her husband, Arif Yunus, were jailed on charges similar to those imposed on Ismayilova. They received terms of eight and a half years and seven years, respectively, the BBC reported.[10] Leyla Yunus is an outspoken and fierce critic of Aliyev and a supporter of reconciliation initiatives between Azerbaijan and Armenia, which were embroiled in a territorial dispute between 1988 and 1994. A fragile woman of 60, Leyla Yunus has lost a significant amount of weight, and is suffering from a number of health issues, according to her lawyer.

And then there is my story—an ugly campaign to discredit me in the eyes of the Azerbaijani people. There were TV shows debating whether I committed treason by promoting reconciliation with Armenia, and some local media outlets labeled me an Armenian spy and said I was working to discredit Aliyev's government while writing in Armenian for a Turkish-Armenian news outlet. Actually, I was an Azerbaijani journalist and commentator, writing occasionally (in fact, in Turkish), about Azerbaijan-related news and events, for a Turkish-Armenian newspaper, *AGOS*, based in Istanbul.

Like Ismayilova, I was labeled a whore by some pro-government journalists and members of a pro-government youth movement known as IRELI, who likewise characterized my mother as a whore who gave birth to a whore. Even my late father was used in a campaign to silence me: In a cartoon that circulated on social media networks, I was depicted in the arms of the Armenian president, alongside a caricature of my father at his own grave with his hand held over his face in shame. On Facebook, people commented by the thousands under pictures with fake descriptions of me, with many users talking about raping me in unimaginable ways, hanging me and punishing me for the crimes I had allegedly committed.

Similar to the sex tape in Ismayilova's case, and the treason accusations in the case of Leyla Yunus, I had to be discredited first before I would receive my public chastisement in the form of allegations of treason and photos of me posted online with captions that read "traitor."

Among the male journalists who have been similarly targeted are Ganimat Zahid and Azer Akhmedov, respectively the editor and the director of the newspaper *Azadlig*, according to Human Rights House, an international group, which also noted that another male journalist was "implicated as having had a homosexual partner in an attempt to harass him."

Given the behavior of the government and individuals and groups operating on its behalf, Ismayilova was aware that her work would likely result in grave personal consequences. Though the government was never linked, some enterprising journalists had paid with their lives. In 2005, Elmar Huseynov, the editor-in-chief of a local magazine that was exposing corruption of the Azerbaijan government, was shot to death on his way home from work in Baku. In 2011, another journalist, Rafig Tagi, was stabbed to death outside his home. In 2015, reporter Rasim Aliyev died in a hospital following a severe beating. In Aliyev's case, the alleged perpetrators have been identified, but none of the other cases have been solved. Years after Huseynov's murder, Ismayilova said in an interview for the film "Amazing Azerbaijan!" that she felt some responsibility. "He was doing it alone ... We all were doing this easy journalism, and he was doing the uncovering," she said.

Given the long-standing attacks on the press in Azerbaijan, Ismayilova said she was disturbed but not surprised when she received the package containing the intimate photos and threat. In response, she decided to go public, which she said was not an easy decision given the inevitable public shaming that would follow. Remarkably, many Azerbaijanis, including some in the country's religious community, defended her, and Ismayilova continued her hard-nosed reporting—until the government played its trump card and imprisoned her.

Though I have not been in direct contact with Ismayilova since then, we communicate through her mother, who sees her in prison, and mutual friends.

Ismayilova is fond of repeating a Vaclav Havel quote that says a life is not worth living that does not involve willingness to sacrifice itself for the sake of values, and she has adhered to that dictum. But it has cost her dearly. And even for those of us who continue to work as journalists, what happened to her and to others like her has exacted a massive toll.

■ ■ ■

Arzu Geybullayeva is a freelance writer based in Istanbul who reports on human rights violations in Azerbaijan.

14. From High Profile to Exile

By Preethi Nallu

Images of Libyans who were killed during the 2011 siege of Misrata in the city's war museum. Female journalists have become acutely aware of their visibility since the uprising.

Source: Iason Athanasiadis

Heba Alshibani did not set out to become a journalist. She had expected to become an academic, as many members of her Libyan family had before the February 2011 uprising that led to the overthrow of Muammar Qaddafi. But when the violence did not abate after Qaddafi's overthrow, Alshibani witnessed events that she felt compelled to record and share. She had no training as a journalist, but had a penchant for exposing "wrongdoings," as she puts it, and felt an almost instinctive need to bring them to light.

So Alshibani began documenting street violence on her cell phone, and soon found herself sharing her videos with local media. That led other outlets to use her reports, and within two years she had worked her way up through Libyan TV in production and with Reuters Libya from a presenter to a manager.

Her ascent required her to take risks in a media environment that had been restrictive for decades, especially for women. "When I ran a show on women's issues, I discussed issues that are never brought up in Libyan households, like rape," she recently recalled from her home in neighboring Malta, where she works as a presenter for Libya's Channel. "I was not going to have a housekeeping show given the times that the country was experiencing."

But Alshibani soon found the story turning on her.

Some Libyan political figures did not take kindly to her "directness," she said. In 2014, she felt compelled to flee after one of them sent her a threatening message through a fellow journalist in Misrata, warning her to leave or face the consequences. She declined to name the official for security reasons, she said, but she did as she was told, under Reuters' direction. Now she covers Libya from abroad, one of many female journalists who have left the country due to continuing instability and a deep-seated cultural conflict that confers upon them a dangerously high profile.

"Everyone including my mentor advised me to leave," Alshibani said. "Finally, one day last year, the security personnel at Reuters came to me and said that I had to evacuate with my husband and children." After three frenetic years of covering assassinations, bombings, migrant crises and the disintegration of the country into "multiple Libyas," her exit was abrupt. She has not returned.

During the four-year battle between rival factions to control Libya's post-revolutionary political landscape, female journalists have become acutely aware of their visibility. Reporting in the unstable country is challenging for anyone, but particularly for women, owing to deep-seated cultural views about gender roles and the efforts of rival factions to coerce the media—especially local outlets—to take sides.

Despite the loosening of Qaddafi-era press restrictions and a proliferation of print publications and TV channels since the uprising, there is no consensus among female journalists interviewed for this story, many of whom declined to be named due to fear of repercussions, about whether journalism in Libya has benefited from Qaddafi's departure or whether women have greater opportunities or are treated equally as professionals today. Qaddafi's government limited the media in the name of stability and order, and since his overthrow, the media has been privatized and opened to a greater diversity of voices. The downside is that the diversity of voices can be inflammatory, and journalists are frequently manipulated or targeted by rival factions—a situation made more dangerous due to the lack of security. Stratified gender roles only add to the risks for female journalists.

The majority of humanitarian organizations,[1] U.N. agencies[2] and foreign media offices[3] left Libya during the summer of 2014, when the highly contested June elections led to renewed clashes between rival militias. Few Western reporters, male or female, have returned.

A decrease in on-the-ground reporting has created a media vacuum, which has been exploited by rival factions who seek to co-opt remaining coverage. Writing for the Committee to Protect Journalists in the 2015 edition of *Attacks on the Press*, Fadil Aliriza noted that facts in post-revolutionary Libya are "hostage to politics" as a result of competing narratives from rival factions. "The extreme polarization of the media landscape, as well as calls for violence through the media and the bullying of journalists by militias, has contributed to a discrediting of the few real remaining journalists who are trying to report the facts," Aliriza wrote.

In April 2015, Reporters Without Borders reported that among the more recent female journalists to flee Libya was Sirine El Amari, who had been France 24's Tripoli correspondent before leaving in

November 2014 due to threats and repeated questioning by authorities in Tripoli about her reports.

Some of the challenges that journalists face in Libya's highly fragmented political terrain are common to many conflict zones, with geography and alliances often governing access to stories and influencing journalists' personal safety. But in Libya, all sides seem to recognize the importance of controlling the media narrative, and tend to see reporters and photographers as integral to the conflict, shaping the narrative and, in some cases, prompting action. Female journalists often represent potent symbols, and inevitably experience an added layer of difficulty.

Even in pre-revolution Libya, being a female reporter was considered "social suicide," according to journalist Manal Bouseifi, who began reporting for a state news outlet in the early 2000s, when media outlets were under Qaddafi's control. Bouseifi contends that such attitudes toward female journalists, especially those choosing to cover politics and hard news, have prevailed among conservative factions and even among many average Libyans.

As in many post-Arab Spring countries, political instability and violence in Libya are frequently reduced by the Western media to a contest between secular and Islamist groups. Though the reality is far more complicated, there is no question that the media is frequently caught in the crossfire. As a result, many female journalists have felt compelled to cover Libya's turmoil from neighboring Tunisia, Egypt or, in Alshibani's case, Malta, which are considered relative safe havens in the region, though with more than a few asterisks attached. Some who fled said they have stopped reporting due to intimidation or lack of direct access to the country.

Alshibani, a member of a prominent Libyan family who married into an equally powerful clan, went into hiding at the start of the 2011 revolution due to her fear of persecution and kidnapping. During that period, many Libyans were afraid to even watch the news on TV for fear of reprisal, she said. "People were huddling around televisions sets and watching news with the volume at its lowest," she recalled.

Today, rival militias and competing government entities seldom agree on anything beyond the importance of controlling the media, which makes the stakes extremely high for journalists, whatever their gender or affiliation, but particularly for women, who stand out. In August 2013, the *Guardian* reported[4] that a journalist had been targeted by gunmen in Benghazi, Libya's second-largest city. Khawlija al-Amami, a presenter for the al-Ahrar TV station, had been shot at by gunmen who pulled up beside her car. She later received a text message warning her to "stop your journalism" or be killed. In April 2015, TV journalist Muftah al-Qatrani[5] was shot dead in his office at Al-Anwar, a privately owned television production company.

An estimated 1,700 armed groups were active in Libya in 2015, according to the Global Conflict Tracker of the Council on Foreign Relations, an independent think tank. One female foreign journalist who has covered Libya since the beginning of the revolution, who asked to remain anonymous for security reasons, said the proliferation of armed groups has led to a "fierce battle for narrative," and that the diversity of voices in Libya has contributed to increasing polarization over those competing narratives. In addition to physical threats, female journalists in Libya report having been socially ostracized, sexually harassed, attacked on social media and generally discriminated against.

Though some female journalists say they were grudgingly tolerated during the Qaddafi era, all journalists were required to toe the government line. Today, they have greater freedom to report, but that freedom is fraught with perils. Comparatively relaxed views of gender roles are typically limited to cities such as Tripoli and Misrata, yet even there, dark undercurrents exist. The majority of the country is dominated by a highly patriarchal society characterized by strict gender segregation.

Journalists interviewed for this story reported that the treatment of female reporters and photographers throughout Libya varies according to whether they are Libyan, Western, Muslim or non–Muslim. The foreign journalist who declined to be identified by name said female Western reporters work under different, unspoken rules and are permitted a code of conduct that would normally breach social norms. She said she has been able to overcome gender limitations; however, while helping train local journalists before the uprising, she observed that "the general confidence levels of young female journalists" was low because they lacked full acceptance and felt negative pressure from their families and communities. In most cases, the female reporters did not receive as much training as the men and were more reticent when conducting interviews with public figures, she said.

"It was often implied that a [Libyan] female journalist's work was somehow less respectable," she said. Because she stood out as an unveiled Western woman, "On one of my last trips I wore *hijab* for the first time, not because I felt the need to adhere to Libyan social norms, but because we knew by then that there were ISIS cells operating in the region and car bombings had become frequent," she said.

Another Western reporter, freelancer Yasmine Ryan, said that despite being treated more leniently than local female reporters, sexism and anxiety over the appearance of the Islamic State in Libya caused her to feel increasingly uncomfortable. Ryan said she is acutely aware of the strategy of ISIS and affiliated groups to employ sex trafficking as a means of "legitimizing women as commodities," which she said has further reduced the presence of female reporters along Libya's eastern and central coast. Ryan still occasionally reports from Libya, when security permits her to do so with relative safety, and she can get a journalist visa.

Rana Jawad, BBC's longtime chief Libya correspondent, also went into temporary hiding following the 2011 uprising, but later resumed reporting and wrote a book, *Tripoli Witness*, a firsthand account of her experiences. Today she covers Libya from Tunis. She said her decision to move from Libya was based on concerns about her and her family's safety, particularly given her high profile as a journalist for the BBC.

Alshibani, who has worked for openly partisan media outlets, said she has observed "extreme hostilities" between members of pro-Islamist and anti-Islamist media who feel extraordinary pressure to adhere to their respective allegiances. She also witnessed female journalists and presenters being coerced into "picking a side in order to continue being employed." Pressure to adhere to conventions is often implicitly gender-based, she said, and of the 40 or so TV channels and more than 100 publications launched in Libya since 2011, "I know of only one other woman in a decision-making role," she said. With a laugh, she added, "Most Libyan men are simply not used to taking orders from women."

Such views of gender are not unique to Libya, but tend to be amplified by the ongoing cultural and political conflict. And in many cases, the conflict has followed female journalists who resorted to self-imposed exile. Alshibani first moved to Tunis, hoping to continue reporting from a relatively safe place and return to Libya when security permitted. Yet even in Tunisia, she was mindful that she could be targeted by operatives representing a Libyan faction, particularly after she heard that a Libyan militia member had been asking around for her contact information. That episode prompted her to move to Malta.

Though Alshibani said she received "veiled" threats, others, including reporter Manal Bouseifi, said they were threatened directly. Bouseifi said she fled her Libyan home after receiving death threats over her "provocative reporting" about the need to re-interpret the *Hadith*, the foundation of Islamic laws.

Bouseifi studied journalism in Libya during the Qaddafi era and began working as an investigative reporter for a Libyan state publication in 2004. Two years later, she said, "I worked on an investigative report on prostitution with a female colleague and we discovered that it was widespread and with many human rights violations. But the story led to backlash against us as women reporting on the topic."

After Qaddafi's fall, "I wrote an article in 2012 about inheritance laws, as I wanted to initiate a discussion on rights of women in political transition and this was the most controversial writing," Bouseifi said. "I quickly discovered that the inheritance law discussion could have led to a slitting of my throat. I am a mother of five children. Four of them are alive. I fled with them." Yet the threats, she said, followed her to Tunis. In September 2015, Bouseifi said she was attacked by a Libyan man on a street who threw coffee in her face. "He said it would not be coffee next time," she added.

The Libyan female journalists who have relocated to Tunis are part of a larger exodus from Libya, owing to Tunisia's geographic proximity and lack of visa restrictions. Nearly one million Libyans have fled to Tunis alone since 2011, according to the Tunisian Ministry of Information. Yet Tunisia is not without its problems, including high unemployment, political division and a tempestuous history with Libya. Bouseifi said she now has plans to relocate to Egypt and to start a human rights publication focused on the women of Libya. She currently manages a group of women inside the country who have been documenting human rights abuses in Libyan prisons and translating reports, such as those by Human Rights Watch, into Arabic for Libyan readers. The women use pseudonyms to protect their identities, she said.

Some Libyan female journalists have chosen to remain in their native country, despite the dangers. Among those going against the grain is a reporter who uses the pen name Mariam Ahmed, who reported for the *Libya Herald* and freelanced for foreign media from her home in Benghazi until October 2015, when she went on hiatus from reporting on "daily death and destruction" because she said the work became too distressing.

Ahmed, who is 22, said she was undaunted by the potential conflict of being a female journalist in a largely conservative community, and has managed to make many high-profile contacts, including among various militias. She said she realizes this makes her something of an anomaly. "The assassinations of 2013 have been replaced by face-to-face battles, and the violence is nonstop," she said. "Women hardly drive anymore, let alone walk on the streets." Because she is often the only female present during tense events, Ahmed is well known, which makes her more visible and, she acknowledged, more vulnerable to attacks. Yet her family supports her work, including her father, who sends her breaking news alerts and helps her find useful sources. "My *baba* [father] told me that if death is to happen, it will happen no matter what, but that I should not live my life in fear," she said.

Like Alshibani, Ahmed felt an overwhelming desire to document the violence around her. "When I wrote my first story in 2012, on the anniversary of the NATO bombing, I found that I could not stop writing," Ahmed said. "But during this period, given that there are no positive stories, I am frustrated."

Asked if she has ever been threatened, Ahmed said the greatest danger she has faced involved being physically caught in crossfire or falling out with a local leader. She said her personal safety and that of her family members hinge heavily on maintaining discretion, asking the right questions and knowing when to refrain.

Another female journalist who held out longer than most is Tunisian Huda Mzioudet, who said that while in Libya, she was mostly treated with respect and even protectiveness. She attributed this to having been veiled and "culturally familiar, yet an outsider."

But, Mzioudet added, increasing danger led her to report on "less adrenaline-driven" stories. Avoiding battle-riddled streets, Mzioudet covered stories on migration, which also required travel to potentially dangerous, remote locations. She remembered one such trip in which a local tribal member who was escorting her through Libya's Sahara Desert region began playing Egyptian love songs on his vehicle's CD player. Sensing that he was coming on to her, "I had to ask myself, what in the world I was doing there with absolutely no protection," she said. Back home in Tunis, she is working on a book chronicling her reporting experiences in Libya for the Brookings Institution.

The sense of gender-based vulnerability, which Mzioudet also experienced while negotiating Tunisia-Libya border crossings, caused her to reevaluate her on-the-ground reporting, she said. During one border crossing, a member of a Libyan militia asked what she was doing in Libya. She lied and told him she was an academic training students, fearing his reaction if he found out she was a journalist. She recalled how her heart raced when his inquiry began to include sexual innuendo and he suggested that she should be spending time "training him in certain acts," as she put it. "I was practically in the middle of nowhere," she said. "As a Tunisian national, I would not count on my government protecting me," she added.

Despite being conspicuous in a male-dominated terrain, many female journalists, both Libyan and non-Libyan, have continued to report on the country, whether from afar, while making periodic forays into Libya, or from within the country itself. Bouseifi noted that her college-age daughter is determined to return to Libya as a journalist and hopes to report in Arabic and English. "It is not an option for her right now, but yes, in the future, when we return," she said. "Insh'allah."

■ ■ ■

Preethi Nallu is a freelance journalist based in Tunis.

15. Males Preferred

By Yaqiu Wang

A network journalist covers delegates arriving at the National People's Congress in Beijing in March 2015. An informal survey on female journalists in China elicited enlightening responses.

Source: Reuters/Jason Lee

I n October 2015, when I solicited Chinese readers' views on gender issues in journalism, one comment spoke volumes about the state of the debate in China: "Women can take advantage of their looks and feminine traits to attract well-known and powerful men to accept their interviews."

The comment, from a male respondent who chose to remain anonymous, reflects a widely held though increasingly antiquated view that, far from facing gender limitations, female journalists in China frequently use sexual appeal to their advantage.

Contrasting with that view was a response from Feng Zhaoyin, a female reporter for Hong Kong-based Initium Media, who said, "As a young female journalist, sometimes older men I interviewed refused to take me seriously. They had the attitude that the newspaper should have sent a man to interview them for such serious topics."

Discussions of the role of female journalists in China often elicit such diametrically opposed viewpoints, and my informal survey was intended to shed light on the topic. In addition to comments gathered through posts on WeChat and Weibo, China's two biggest social media platforms, I interviewed several former and current female and male journalists from TV stations, news websites and newspapers in China. Though not a scientific survey, the responses I received were both enlightening and contradictory. Clearly, gender bias is a volatile subject in China today.

A male former website editor for Phoenix TV, Zhuo Yuzhen (@ zhuoyuzhen), said he "rarely heard of" instances of sexual harassment during his tenure in the field of journalism. Yet Zhao Sile, a female freelance journalist, told me, "Instances of female journalists being harassed? How many and how big of a name do you want?"

Such perceptual disconnect illustrates the kinds of challenges Chinese female journalists face.

China's news industry is vast. In addition to countless news websites, blogs and social media accounts that are constantly being shut down and re-created, mainland China in 2014 reported having 1,915 print newspapers with a circulation of 132 million, and by late 2015, there were more than 208,000 journalists with press cards, of which 47 percent were women. Some reports estimate that the total number[1] of journalists, including those who do not hold press cards, may actually exceed one million, with a little over half of them being women. Those numbers represent a steady uptick in female journalists.

Still, the increase in the number of working female journalists during the past two decades does not correspond to the high percentage of female journalism graduates today. For years, women have far outnumbered men among journalism school graduates in China. In 2006, 65 percent of master's students in journalism at Sichuan University, one of China's most prominent universities, were women.[2] In 2012, two-thirds of all graduate students at the Communication University of China, among China's foremost media education institutions, were women.[3] Eighty percent of the 245 journalism students in the class of 2017 at Anhui University, a major public university, are women.[4]

The question is: Why do so many women with journalism degrees not become working journalists? The answer may have something to do with those divergent approaches to the role of gender in journalism.

China's press environment is notoriously stifling, with frequent government interference and stringent government control. Female journalists face additional cultural and political barriers. Within the realm of allowed topics, some journalists have been able to publish important work and receive recognition, but most of them are men. Many of the journalists who offered their input on the topic believe the barriers female journalists face, including gender discrimination in hiring, are part of the reason there has not been a greater increase in the number of female journalists despite the growing number of female journalism graduates.

Gender discrimination in hiring for many professions is widespread in China. According to a 2014 survey, 86.6 percent of recent female college graduates said they had been subjected to at least one instance of gender-based discrimination when seeking jobs.[5] Job announcements sometimes include the notation "males only" or "males preferred," or require women to have a higher degree for the same position. This happens despite several laws prohibiting gender discrimination in employment.

"Usually, organizations don't want to hire women who have plans to have children soon," Zhuo Yuzhen said. "I know this is wrong but

I have to admit that I took applicants' family plans into consideration while I was recruiting new journalists. Think about it: Not long after you hire someone, she goes on to take six months of maternity leave."

Li Sipan, a former reporter for *Southern Metropolis* and now a Ph.D. student in sociology at Macau University, told me that female journalists have made inroads and sparked resistance. Many newspapers, she said, have a preference for male journalists but struggle to find qualified male candidates. "Over the years, I've heard many human resources people in newspapers complaining about there being too many female journalists and they want to recruit more male journalists," she said. "However, if you look at the applicants' resumes, a lot of female applicants graduated from overseas universities and top-tier Chinese universities. You don't see many male applicants from reputable schools." Though Li did not offer any research to back up the claim, she added, "The quality of female applicants overall is much better than males."

There has likewise been resistance to career advancement for female journalists. A 2013 survey of more than 600 female journalists in Shanghai found that 60 percent believed women are discriminated against when being considered for promotions.[6] A 2011 survey conducted by the International Women's Media Foundation found that women held only 7.7 percent of top-level management positions in Chinese news companies.[7]

"The distrust in women's ability to lead is deeply rooted," said Li Sipan, who is also a women's rights advocate. "I have a good friend who was a key editorial member in a fashion and lifestyle media company. She used to be annoyed by my feminist theories. One time, her company was going to publish a new magazine. She thought, given her expertise and experience, she would be selected to lead the magazine. But instead of choosing her to be the editor-in-chief, the company leadership brought in a man who clearly had less aptitude than her to be her boss. She told me that at that moment, she suddenly realized what gender discrimination is and what a glass ceiling is."

When discussing female role models in Chinese journalism, two names often come up: Hu Shuli and Jiang Yiping. Hu founded *Caijing* and *Caixin*, two leading financial magazines, and was listed among *Time* magazine's "Top 100 Influential People" in 2011 and *Forbes*' "100 Most Powerful Women" in 2014. Jiang, the former deputy

editor-in-chief of Southern Media Group, a liberal-leaning media con-
glomerate in Guangdong province, is known for pioneering critical
political op-ed writing in China.

While the professional ascents of women such as Hu and Jiang
are typically viewed as extraordinary, they are often attributed to the
women's personal connections. "Female journalists like Hu and Jiang
are extremely talented and hard-working women, but at the same time
they are also the children of Communist Party leaders," said a female
reporter who asked to remain anonymous because she knows Hu
and Jiang personally. "It's almost impossible to achieve what they've
achieved in journalism if you are not the daughter or wife of a powerful man."

Hu's maternal grandfather was a well-known translator and an
editor of *Shen Bao*, one of the earliest and most influential newspapers in modern China.[8] Her mother was a senior editor at *Worker's
Daily* in Beijing. Her father was part of a Communist cadre in a trade
union. Jiang's father was a Communist revolutionary who fought in
the country's civil war and later became one of the youngest leaders in
Guangdong province.[9]

Hu and Jiang did not respond to emails inquiring whether their
connections helped them to overcome gender bias.

In general, female journalists receive substantially fewer accolades and major journalism awards in China, partly because they tend
to be limited in the topics they are assigned to cover, but sometimes,
according to one journalist, due to overt gender bias. A 2011 study of
two official journalist prizes,[10] the China Journalism Award and the
Changjiang and Taofen Award, found that women constituted 19.6
percent of the winners and less than 7 percent of the judges between
1991 and 2009.[11]

"I once did an investigative story on sexual harassment," recalled
one female reporter who asked to remain anonymous due to fear of
repercussions. "After we ran the story, the victim went on to take the
case to court and eventually won. It was big news that year. But I only
got the bronze medal in a year-end competition within our newspaper.
I feel my reporting at least was as good as my male colleague's that
won the gold medal, and perhaps even better given that my subject was
more original."

Negative Chinese stereotypes of women as emotional and less logical and analytical can also cost women professional opportunities and hinder their career development. "The Chinese media industry's most pronounced value statements often contain words like 'rational' and 'constructive,'" said a veteran journalist, now a doctoral student in communication science at University of Wisconsin-Madison who goes by the pen name Hongniang Dingdang. "What are qualities of a good journalist—emotionally strong, rational and objective. These are all considered traits that are inherently associated with men in our society. Men benefit from the system for just being men."

The journalists I interviewed agreed that hard news stories— including disasters and issues related to politics, economics and the military—are more often assigned to male journalists. Coverage of family issues, fashion and entertainment—"soft news"—are more often assigned to female journalists. The hard news covered by men typically translates into the type of "big news" that results in professional recognition.

"I remember in 2003, when China launched its first manned space shuttle, journalists sent to Jiuquan, where the launch took place, were all men," Hongniang Dingdang recalled. "During the 2008 Sichuan earthquake, most of the journalists at the earthquake epicenter aftermath scene were men. A few female journalists who went there were able to interview soldiers of the rescue crew. Male journalists complained that their female counterparts got the opportunities because male soldiers like to talk to women. I thought to myself: Why don't you guys think about how the vast majority of journalists given the opportunity to be at the scene are men in the first place?" Only 10 of the 41 journalists *Southern Metropolis* sent to cover the earthquake were women.[12]

Some male journalists defended such division of labor because it protects female journalists from danger and hardship. Xu Honggang, an editor at *Southern Metropolis*, said, "Reporting on events like traffic accidents and fire accidents requires energy. Men are physically stronger."

"If I were to make the decision, I would definitely not send a woman to go undercover to cover underground kidney trading," said Zhuo Yuzhen, referring to an award-winning story on an organ trafficking ring in Zhejiang province in 2012. "As the boss, you are responsible for your subordinates' safety."[13]

Among female journalists who responded to my online survey, some wrote about the gender issues they encountered in their careers, such as sexual harassment and discrimination in promotion decisions, while others discounted the notion of gender discrimination in journalism and said both men and women play on their respective strengths in reporting. Many male commenters, whether journalists or non-journalists, doubted the validity of the question itself, saying that female journalists are actually at an advantage. According to one commenter, "People are more acceptable to female journalists approaching them." Another wrote, "Women, especially good-looking women, can get valuable intelligence easier." And one alleged, "Women can sleep with male leaders to get what they want while men can't."

When I asked female journalists their opinions of such views, Zhang Xin, a former reporter for Chongqing TV who now lives and works in Europe, said she was familiar with such accusations. "People often think women who work in TV broadcasting all sleep around to get ahead," Zhang said. "There are such cases, but they are definitely not as common as many people think. We work hard and late and our social circle is rather small."

Li Sipan said the idea that women can use sex appeal for career advancement purposes is unrealistic. "To be a good journalist ultimately depends on the quality of your writing. I've never known anyone who can gain professional recognition and respect as a journalist by sleeping with whoever."

Feng Zhaoyin said, "If women use their femininity to approach male interviewees, male journalists use their 'brotherly affinity' to get close to their sources as well."

Zhao Sile said the perception that female journalists use their femininity to their advantage could be influenced by several recent high-profile scandals in China concerning government officials and female TV anchors. For example, in 2013, a series of anchors at China's state-owned TV broadcaster, CCTV, were reportedly[14] under investigation for illicit involvement with top Communist Party leader Zhou Yongkang, former head of the state police, judiciary, and foreign and domestic intelligence services.

Li Sipan said the stigmatization of female journalists could also be due to men feeling threatened by female journalists' increasing numbers and prominence. Although the number of female journalists has not kept pace with the number of journalism graduates, both are increasing. And despite the fact that fewer female journalists receive awards and accolades, their prominence is slowly growing.

Lüqiu Luwei, formerly a journalist for Phoenix TV and now a Ph.D. student in the College of Communications at Pennsylvania State University, became a household name in China in 2003 when she became the first female Chinese war correspondent to cover the Iraq War. Dubbed "The Rose in the War Zone," she received extensive media attention, though much of it focused on her gender rather than her work.

"It's a reflection of our time," Lüqiu said of the emphasis on her gender. She compared it with journalist Christiane Amanpour covering the Gulf War in the early 1990s. "I don't really mind people emphasizing my gender identity," she said, "but when there is an opportunity, I always raise the point that what matters in reporting is my experience, not my gender."

Lüqiu believes the novelty of women reporting in dangerous situations is fading. "I'm seeing changes," she said. "When media outlets use females reporting from conflict zones as a selling point nowadays, Chinese viewers no longer buy it."

■ ■ ■

Yaqiu Wang is CPJ's Northeast Asia correspondent. She has a master of arts in international affairs from George Washington University. Her articles on civil society and human rights in China have appeared in publications including Foreign Policy, The Atlantic, *and* China Change.

16. Compassion, Strength, Hugs

By Kathleen Carroll

The author, right, with veteran AP correspondent Kathy Gannon at CPJ's 2015 International Press Freedom Awards.

Source: Barbara Nitke for CPJ

I am a hugger. Maybe it's my Texas heritage, but the value of wrapping people in a warm embrace at the right time has stayed with me, like a hint of twang, in the 40 years since I left the state. And hugs have been just the right thing many times during the decades that the safety of journalists has been a big part of my working life.

When journalists are headed to their first assignment in a tough place, no matter how much training they've had, no matter how many serious talks about preparation and assessing risk they've had, it just doesn't seem right to send them off with a sober handshake. I need to put an arm or two around their shoulders.

People coming home get hugs of welcome and thanks, newbies and seasoned veterans alike. Maybe especially seasoned veterans, who carry so many horrible images and experiences that most of us can know only through their work. And I take hugs with me (calibrated for different cultures) when visiting Associated Press staff around the world, one of the great privileges of my life.

It's clear that I can hug people because I am a woman. A red-haired, married, middle-aged working mother with a loud-ish laugh. Change one thing—gender—and imagine a loud-ish, red-haired, middle-aged man in a suit opening his arms wide as he approaches.

Yeah. It doesn't feel quite the same.

Is hugging a leadership tool? The very question makes human resources executives queasy. After all, physical contact in the workplace is usually more of a problem than a solution.

When we're asking people to work in places where every decision they make must be weighed against the potential threat to their lives, we need all the tools we can muster.

That's why, in the right circumstances, hugs are essential. Nurturing, too.

Now that's a loaded word for leaders who are women because it's one of the clichéd descriptions that most of us have heard at one time or another.

It's part of the caricature that makes many women bristle.

You know: "She's soft and nurturing." The opposite of "She's bossy and too tough."

In my experience, though, you need every trait available on the soft-tough continuum when you are looking after people who work in difficult places. You need intuition and heart when listening to them.

You need to be firm about assignments and safety protocols. You need to be organized enough to have plans ready in case something goes wrong. Then you need to be fast, relentless, tough and if, God forbid, something does go wrong, tender.

How does anyone—woman or man—learn how to do that?

Sadly, most of us learn it by brute experience, which is frustrating, terrifying, rewarding, occasionally exhilarating and always very hard.

Good training and tools are increasingly available to journalists who work in dangerous places, even for those who are most imperiled … the ones covering the places where they live.

There is precious little training for bosses.

Some of us have good informal networks with colleagues, even competitors, who face the same challenges. Those informal networks, and the splendid folks at CPJ, are a resource when things go wrong.

Because the dangers are growing every year, we have to ask if that is enough.

Shouldn't we do more to prepare newsroom leaders in charge of journalists in dodgy places?

In other professions, leadership training includes extensive time with case studies. There's not much of that around safety issues in journalism, though. The hard-won wisdom lives with individuals and sometimes in pockets of news organizations.

A number of things get in the way of the kind of sharing that makes an effective case study. First, because lives are at stake, people can be reluctant to share details of how a sticky situation was resolved, even when the resolution is a good one.

There are legal risks—risks to the channels invoked while trying to get the journalist out of danger and other sensitive details that a company may choose not to share.

The employer isn't the only person with a stake here. Family members almost always have a say, and sometimes they disagree among themselves. Once safe, the journalist may have a view.

As a result, lessons often are confined to the news organization that has been through the ordeal.

The reasons are understandable, but it means other leaders often do not benefit from the experiences of those who've been in those difficult positions before.

So for now, leaders often have to rely on the experience of their own organization when a journalist is wounded or killed. And they have to rely on intuition.

If you've walked that path, you know you must put aside your feelings and summon calm strength to take care of your stricken journalist, their family and their peers in the organization.

You must help them work through fear, sorrow and all the other raw feelings they will have. You must help them gather to gain strength from each other.

On those most dreadful days, your most effective leadership tools will be a nurturing compassion, strength and, at least for me, an endless supply of quiet hugs.

■ ■ ■

Kathleen Carroll, *vice chair of CPJ's board of directors, is executive editor and senior vice president of The Associated Press.*

Notes

Introduction Breaking the Silence

1. Kleeman, Jenny. "Why Discourage Women From Reporting on the Tahrir Square Protests?" *The Guardian*, November 25, 2011, http://www.theguardian.com/commentisfree/2011/nov/25/tahrir-square-women-reporting.

2. Reporters Without Borders. "Media Urged to Prioritize Safety After Another Sexual Assault on Woman Reporter," November 25, 2011, http://en.rsf.org/egypte-media-urged-to-prioritize-safety-after-another-sexual-assault-on-woman-reporter-25-11-2011,41465.html.

3. Wolfe, Lauren. "The Silencing Crime: Sexual Violence and Journalists," Committee to Protect Journalists, July 2, 2011, https://cpj.org/reports/2011/06/silencing-crime-sexual-violence-journalists.php.

4. Barton, Alana, and Hannah Storm. "Violence and Harassment Against Women in the News Media," International Women's Media Foundation, March 10, 2014, https://www.iwmf.org/our-research/journalist-safety/violence-and-harassment-against-women-in-the-news-media-a-global-picture/.

5. Logan, Lara. Interview with Scott Pelley, "Lara Logan Breaks Silence on Cairo Assault," *60 Minutes*, May 1, 2011, http://www.cbsnews.com/news/lara-logan-breaks-silence-on-cairo-assault/4/.

1. The Sadness of May the 25th

1. Committee to Protect Journalists, Ann K. Cooper (executive director). Letter to Andrés Pastrana Arango (president of Colombia) sent via facsimile May 31, 2000, https://cpj.org/2000/05/colombia-reporter-kidnapped-tortured-after-coverin.php.

2. Casa de la Mujer, Oxfam, and UK Ministry of Foreign Affairs. "Executive Summary: First Survey on the Prevalence of Sexual Violence Against Women in the Context of the Colombia Armed Conflict, 2001–2009," 2011, http://www.usofficeoncolombia.org/uploads/application-pdf/2011-03-23-Report-English.pdf.

3. Why a Troll Trolls

1. Pew Research Center. "Online Harassment," October 2014, http://www.pewinternet.org/files/2014/10/PI_OnlineHarassment_72815.pdf.

2. International Women's Media Foundation. "Intimidation, Threats, and Abuse," *Violence and Harassment Against Women in the News Media: A Global Picture*, 2014, http://www.iwmf.org/intimidation-threats-and-abuse/.

3. Parkin, Simon. "Zoe Quinn's Depression Quest," *The New Yorker*, September 9, 2014, http://www.newyorker.com/tech/elements/zoe-quinns-depression-quest.

4. New Statesman. "What Is the Overton Window?" *New Statesman*, April 27, 2015, http://www.newstatesman.com/politics/2015/04/what-overton-window.

5. Buckels, Erin E., Paul D. Trapnell and Delroy L. Paulhus. "Trolls Just Want to Have Fun," *Personality and Individual Differences* 67 (September 2014): 97–102, doi: 10.1016/j.paid.2014.01.016.

6. Dakers, Marion. "'Troll Insurance' to Cover the Cost of Internet Bullying," *The Telegraph*, December 9, 2015, http://www.telegraph.co.uk/finance/newsbysector/banksandfinance/insurance/12041832/Troll-insurance-to-cover-the-cost-of-internet-bullying.html.

7. Phillips, Whitney. *This Is Why We Can't Have Nice Things: Mapping the Relationship Between Online Trolling and Mainstream Culture.* Cambridge, MA: MIT Press, 2015.

8. West, Lindy. "Ask Not for Whom the Bell Trolls; It Trolls for Thee," *This American Life*, Episode 545, January 23, 2015.

9. Blunden, Mark. "Caroline Criado-Perez: How I Won My Banknote Battle ... and Defied Rape Threat Trolls," *Evening Standard*, November 26, 2015, http://www.standard.co.uk/news/london/caroline-criadoperez-how-i-won-my-banknote-battle-and-defied-rape-threat-trolls-a3123956.html.

10. BBC.com. "Two Guilty Over Abusive Tweets to Caroline Criado-Perez," January 7, 2014, http://www.bbc.co.uk/news/uk-25641941.

11. BBC Newsbeat. "Twitter Troll Isabella Sorley Reads Out Her Abusive Tweets," *Radio One Newsbeat*, November 17, 2014, https://youtu.be/nayMC_urrCo.

4. Preparing for the Worst

1. Committee to Protect Journalists. Database of Killed Journalists, 2016, https://cpj.org/killed/2015.

2. Committee to Protect Journalists. Database of Killed Journalists, 2016, https://cpj.org/killed/2015/murder.php.

3. International Women's Media Foundation and the International News Safety Institute. "Violence and Harassment Against Women in the News Media," March 10, 2014, http://www.iwmf.org/our-research/journalist-safety/violence-and-harassment-against-women-in-the-news-media-a-global-picture/flipbook/.

4. Moisse, Katie. "CBS Reporter Lara Logan Opens Up About Tahrir Square Attack," ABC News, May 2, 2011, http://abcnews.go.com/Health/MindMoodNews/cbs-reporter-lara-logan-opens-tahrir-square-assault/story?id=13492964.

5. Rivers, Dan. "UK Journalist Assaulted in Tahrir Square: 'Please Make It Stop,'" June 28, 2011, http://www.cnn.com/2012/06/27/world/meast/egypt-journalist-assaulted/

6. Abramovitch, Seth. "Dutch Journalist Sexually Assaulted by Protestors in Tahrir Square," *The Hollywood Reporter*, July 2, 2013, http://www.hollywoodreporter.com/news/dutch-journalist-sexually-assaulted-by-578661.

7. Wolfe, Lauren. "NYT's Lynsey Addario on Libya Sexual Assault," Committee to Protect Journalists blog, April 4, 2011, https://cpj.org/blog/2011/04/qa-nyts-lynsey-addario-on-libya-sexual-assault.php.

8. Addario, Lynsey. *It's What I Do: A Photographer's Life of Love and War*. New York: Penguin, 2015.

9. Smyth, Frank. "Journalist Security Guide: Covering the News in a Dangerous and Changing World," Committee to Protect Journalists, 2012, https://cpj.org/reports/2012/04/journalist-security-guide.php.

10. Rory Peck Trust. "Freelance Resources: Safety & Security," August 2013, https://rorypecktrust.org/resources/safety-and-security.

5. LGBT Reporting in Africa

1. Kushner, Jacob, and Anthony Langat. "Anti-LGBT Groups Are Making Inroads Across East Africa," *Global Post*, June 15, 2015, http://www.globalpost.com/article/6580371/2015/06/12/anti-lgbt-groups-making-inroads-across-east-africa.

7. Double Exposure

1. Erasing 76 Crimes. "Africa" category archive, 2016, http://76crimes.com/category/africa-sub-saharan/.

2. *Kuchu Times*. "Attacks on LGBTI Persons on the Rise Within Kampala," October 27, 2015, https://www.kuchutimes.com/2015/10/violent-attacks-on-lgbti-persons-on-the-rise-within-kampala/.

3. Brydum, Sunnivie. "LGBT Ugandans Attacked, Killed as Tabloid Lists 'Top 200 Homos,'" *Advocate*, February 25, 2014, http://www.advocate.com/world/2014/02/25/lgbt-ugandans-attacked-tabloid-lists-top-200-homos.

4. Johnston, Chris. "Uganda Drafts New Anti-Gay Laws," *The Guardian*, November 8, 2014, http://www.theguardian.com/world/2014/nov/08/uganda-drafts-anti-gay-laws-prison-promotion-homosexuality.

5. Agence France-Presse in Kampala. "Gay Ugandans Hope New Magazine Will Rewrite Wrongs by Tackling Homophobia," *The Guardian*, February 9, 2011, http://www.theguardian.com/world/2015/feb/09/uganda-gay-magazine-homophobia.

6. Ennis, Dawn. "LGBT Ugandans Launch Magazine 'Our Voices, Our Stories, Our Lives,'" *Advocate*, February 11, 2015, http://www .advocate.com/uganda/2015/02/11/lgbt-ugandans-launch-magazine-share-our-voices-our-stories-our-lives.

7. Erasing 76 Crimes. "79 Countries Where Homosexuality Is Illegal," December 3, 2015, http://76crimes.com/76-countries-where-homosexuality-is-illegal/.

8. Transgender Europe. "Trans Murder Monitoring" project, 2015, http:// transrespect.org/en/research/trans-murder-monitoring/.

9. Jacques, Juliet. "On the 'Dispute' Between Radical Feminism and Trans People," *New Statesman*, August 6, 2014, http://www.newstatesman.com/ juliet-jacques/2014/08/dispute-between-radical-feminism-and-trans-people.

10. O'Neill, Brendan. "Call Me Caitlyn or Else: The Rise of Authoritarian Transgender Politics," *The Spectator*, June 2, 2015, http://blogs.spectator.co.uk/ 2015/06/call-me-caitlyn-or-else-the-rise-of-authoritarian-transgender-politics/.

11. McCormick, Joseph Patrick. "Columnist Julie Burchill: Trans Women Are Just 'Big White Blokes Who Have Cut Their Cocks Off,'" *Pink News*, March 11, 2014, http://www.pinknews.co.uk/2014/03/11/columnist-julie-burchill-trans-women-just-big-white-blokes-cut-genitals-cant-call-women/.

12. BBC News. "Stag Gore Victim Dr Kate Stone Says Press 'trampled on private life,'" May 14, 2014, http://www.bbc.com/news/uk-england-27405267.

13. Committee to Protect Journalists. "Attacks on the Press: Uganda," 2013, https://cpj.org/2014/02/attacks-on-the-press-in-2013-uganda.php.

14. Karungi, Beyonce. "Human Rights! In Whose Lens? The Agony of a Transgender Woman in Uganda," *Kuchu Times*, September 10, 2015, https://www.kuchutimes.com/2015/09/human-rights-in-whose-lens-the-agony-of-a-transgender-woman-in-uganda/.

15. Agence France-Presse in Kampala. "Gay Ugandans Hope New Magazine Will Rewrite Wrongs by Tackling Homophobia," *The Guardian*, February 9, 2015, http://www.theguardian.com/world/2015/feb/09/ uganda-gay-magazine-homophobia.

16. Ibid.

17. Ibid., 4.

18. Sanghani, Radhika. "Troll Pays Twitter to Promote Message Telling Transgender People to Commit Suicide," *Telegraph*, May 21, 2015, http://www.telegraph.co.uk/women/womens-life/11619984/Troll-pays-Twitter-to-promote-message-telling-trans-people-to-commit-suicide.html.

8. Combating Digital Harassment

1. Organization for Security and Co-operation in Europe. "Communiqué 02/2015 on the Growing Safety Threat to Female Journalists Online," 2015, http://www.osce.org/fom/139186.

2. Organization for Security and Co-operation in Europe. "Recommendations on Countering Online Abuse of Female Journalists," 2015, http://www.osce.org/fom/193556?download=ture.

3. Global Media Monitoring Project. "Who Makes the News?" 2015, http://cdn.agilitycms.com/who-makes-the-news/Imported/reports_2010/global/gmmp_global_report_en.pdf.

9. Responding to Internet Abuse

1. Freitas, Ana. "Nerds e Machismo: Por que mulheres não são bem vindas nos foruns e chans," *HuffPost Brasil*, February 2, 2015, http://www.brasilpost.com.br/ana-freitas/nerds-e-machismo-porque-m_b_6598174.html.

2. Internet Governance Forum. Best Practice Forum (BPF) on Online Abuse and Gender-Based Violence Against Women, 2015, http://www.intgovforum.org/cms/documents/best-practice-forums/539-draft-jp-bpf-women/file.

3. International Womens Media Foundation and International News Safety Institute. "Violence and Harassment Against Women in the News Media: A Global Picture," 2014, https://www.iwmf.org/wp-content/uploads/2014/03/Violence-and-Harassment-against-Women-in-the-News-Media.pdf.

4. Association for Progressive Communications. "End Violence: Women's Rights and Safety Online," 2014, https://www.apc.org/en/node/15007/.

5. Rutkin, Aviva. "The Fight Back Against Rape and Death Threats Online," *New Scientist*, December 10, 2014, https://www.newscientist.com/article/mg22429996.000-the-fight-back-against-rape-and-death-threats-online/.

6. GenderIT.org. "Internet Intermediaries and Violence Against Women Online: User Policies and Redress Framework of Facebook, Twitter and YouTube," 2014, http://www.genderit.org/resources/internet-intermediaries-and-violence-against-women-online-user-policies-and-redress-framew.

7. Ibid., 5.

8. Nazish, Kiran. "Threats to Pakistan's Women Journalists," *The New York Times*, October 23, 2015, http://kristof.blogs.nytimes.com/2015/10/23/threats-to-pakistans-women-journalists/?_r=0#more-13311.

9. Global Voices. "The 'Beauty' of Russian Homophobia," April 20, 2015, https://globalvoices.org/2015/04/20/the-beauty-of-russian-homophobia/.

10. Ibid., 5.

11. Ibid., 5.

12. Ibid., 2.

13. Kaye, David. "Report of the Special Rapporteur on the Promotion and Protection of the Right to Freedom of Opinion and Expression," United Nations Human Rights Council, May 22, 2015, http://www.ohchr.org/EN/Issues/FreedomOpinion/Pages/CallForSubmission.aspx.

14. O'Brien, Danny. "China's Name Registration Will Only Aid Cybercriminals," Committee to Protect Journalists blog, December 28, 2012, https://cpj.org/blog/2012/12/chinas-name-registration-will-aid-not-hinder-cyber.php.

15. O'Brien, Danny. "Google+, Real Names and Real Problems," Committee to Protect Journalists blog, January 26, 2012, https://cpj.org/blog/2012/01/google-real-names-and-real-problems.php.

16. Ibid., 8

17. Pew Research Center. "Online Harassment," October 22, 2014, http://www.pewinternet.org/2014/10/22/online-harassment/.

18. Harper, Randi. "Good Game Auto Blocker," Randi.io blog, April 17, 2015, http://blog.randi.io/good-game-auto-blocker/.

12. Fighting Words

1. Laville, Sandra. "UN Aid Worker Suspended for Leaking Report on Child Abuse by French Troops," *The Guardian*, April 29, 2015, http://www.theguardian.com/world/2015/apr/29/un-aid-worker-suspended-leaking-report-child-abuse-french-troops-car.

2. Askin, Kelly. "Prosecuting Wartime Rape and Other Gender-Related Crimes Under International Law: Extraordinary Advances, Enduring Obstacles," *Berkeley Journal of International Law* 21(2), 2003, http://scholarship.law.berkeley.edu/cgi/viewcontent.cgi?article=1240&context=bjil.

3. Swiss, Shana, and Joan E. Giller. "Rape as a Crime of War: A Medical Perspective," *The Journal of the American Medical Association* 270(5): 612–615, 1993, http://jama.jamanetwork.com/article.aspx?articleid=407731.

4. BBC News. "UN's CAR Envoy Gaye Sacked Over Peacekeeper Abuse Claims," August 12, 2015, http://www.bbc.com/news/world-africa-33890664.

5. C-SPAN. "U.N. Peacekeeping," December 9, 2015, http://www.c-span.org/video/?401798-1/hearing-un-peacemaking&start=1638.

6. Gladstone, John, and Somini Sengupta. "U.N. Wants Sexual Abuse Reported Immediately," *The New York Times*, December 22, 2015, http://www.nytimes.com/2015/12/23/world/un-wants-sexual-abuse-reported-immediately.html?mwrsm=Facebook&_r=0.

7. Wolfe, Lauren. "A Miserable Mystery in Congo," *Foreign Policy*, April 9, 2015, http://foreignpolicy.com/2015/04/09/a-miserable-mystery-in-congo/.

8. Committee to Protect Journalists. "Sudan Journalists Who Report on Rape Charged With Crimes," June 6, 2011, https://cpj.org/2011/06/sudan-journalists-who-report-on-rape-charged-with.php.

9. Committee to Protect Journalists. "Journalist Arrested for Interviewing Reported Rape Victim," January 11, 2013, https://cpj.org/2013/01/journalist-arrested-for-interviewing-reported-rape.php.

10. Committee to Protect Journalists. "Nigerian journalist threatened for alleging rape at a boys' school," October 30, 2015, https://cpj.org/2015/10/nigerian-journalist-threatened-for-alleging-rape-a.php.

11. Committee to Protect Journalists. "Mae Azango, Liberia: 2012 CPJ International Press Freedom Awardee," 2012, https://cpj.org/awards/2012/mae-azango-liberia.php.

12. Committee to Protect Journalists, Joel Simon (executive director). Letter to Ellen Johnson Sirleaf (president of Liberia) sent via facsimile March 13, 2012, https://cpj.org/2012/03/cpj-urges-liberia-to-protect-threatened-journalist.php.

13. Nkanga, Peter, and CPJ Africa Program. "In Liberia, Journalist Mae Azango Moves Nation," Committee to Protect Journalists blog, April 5, 2012, https://cpj.org/blog/2012/04/in-liberia-journalist-mae-azango-moves-a-nation.php.

14. Committee to Protect Journalists. "DRC Government Bans Screening of Documentary on Rape," September 11, 2015, https://cpj.org/2015/09/drc-government-bans-screening-of-documentary-on-ra.php.

13. Harassed and Jailed

1. Committee to Protect Journalists. "Khadija Ismayilova," Press Uncuffed campaign, 2015, https://cpj.org/campaigns/pressuncuffed/khadija-ismayilova.php.

2. Open Democracy. "Dynasty and Democracy in Azerbaijan," December 5, 2003, https://www.opendemocracy.net/democracy-protest/article_1626.jsp.

3. Ismayilova, Khadija. "Aliyevs Azerbaijani Empire Grows as Daughter Joins the Game," RFERL, August 13, 2010, http://www.rferl.org/content/Aliyevs_Azerbaijani_Empire_Grows_As_Daughter_Joins_The_Game/2127137.html.

4. Ismayilova, Khadija. "Azerbaijan President's Family Benefits From Eurovision Hall Construction," RFERL, January 19, 2010, http://www.rferl.org/content/azerbaijan_first_family_build_eurovision_arena/24575761.html.

5. Ismayilova, Khadija. "Azerbaijan Goldfield Contract Awarded to President's Family," RFERL, May 3, 2012, http://www.rferl.org/content/azerbaijan_gold-field_contract_awarded_to_presidents_family/24569192.html.

6. Human Rights House. "Azerbaijan: In Solidarity with Khadija Ismayilova," March 16, 2012, http://humanrightshouse.org/Articles/17785.html

7. Human Rights House Foundation. "Azerbaijan Arrests One More Critical Voice, Khadija Ismayilova," December 5, 2014, http://humanrightshouse.org/Articles/20612.html.

8. Radio Free Europe/Radio Liberty. "Azerbaijan: Ismayilova, IFERL New Charges," January 19, 2016, http://www.rferl.org/content/azerbaijan-ismayilova-rferl-new-charges/26848343.html.

9. BBC News. "Azerbaijan Journalist Khadija Ismayilova Jailed in Baku," September 1, 2015, http://www.bbc.com/news/world-europe-34116812.

10. BBC News. "Azerbaijan Jails Rights Activists Leyla and Arif Yunus," August 13, 2015, http://www.bbc.com/news/world-europe-33905690.

14. From High Profile to Exile

1. IRIN. "Libya Insecurity Forces Aid Workers to Leave," *The Guardian*, August 10, 2014, http://www.theguardian.com/global-development/2014/aug/10/libya-insecurity-aid-workers-leave.

2. Al-Warfalli, Ayman, and Feras Bosalum. "U.N. Pulls Staff Out of Libya as Clashes Kill 13, Close Airports," Reuters, July 15, 2014, http://www.reuters.com/article/2014/07/15/us-libya-violence-idUSKBN0FJ0ZT20140715.

3. Aliriza, Fadil. "Lack of Media Coverage Compounds Violence in Libya," Committee to Protect Journalists, April 2015, https://cpj.org/2015/04/attacks-on-the-press-lack-of-media-coverage-compounds-violence-in-libya.php.

4. Stephen, Chris, "Libyan Journalist Shot as Militants Target Media in Benghazi," *The Guardian*, August 13, 2013, http://www.theguardian.com/world/2013/aug/13/libyan-journalist-shot-militants-benghazi.

5. Committee to Protect Journalists. "Muftah al-Qatrani," April 23, 2015, https://cpj.org/killed/2015/muftah-al-qatrani.php.

15. Males Preferred

1. China News Service. "调查称国内九成以上基层新闻从业者月收入低于1万," [Report Claims over 90 Percent of Entry-level Journalists' Monthly Income is Lower than 10, 000 RMB], China News Service, September 13, 2014, http://www.chinanews.com/gn/2014/09-13/6588382.shtml

2. Lin Lin. "女性报道者的角色嬗变—从凤凰卫视伊拉克战争报道谈起," [The Change of the Role of Female Reporters – from Phoenix TV's Coverage of the Iraq War], *Modern Media*, April 1, 2014,http://www.chinanews.com/n/2004-04-01/26/420614.html

3. Wang Xiaobo. "大学男女比例严重失调 专家称国内教育适合女生," [Serious Gender Imbalance in College, Experts say Chinese Education is Suitable for Women], *Yanzhao Metropolis*, July 25, 2012,http://news.sciencenet.cn/html-news/2012/7/267382.shtm

4. Ding Li and Luo Min. "高校男女比例失衡 或影响学生心理及未来就业," [Gender Imbalance in College May Affect Students' Psychology and Future Employment], *Anhui News*, September 14, 2013, http://ah.anhuinews.com/system/2013/09/14/006074205.shtml

5. Li Lin. "女大学生找工作因是女性三次被拒 性别歧视仍严重," [Female College Graduate's Job Application Rejected Thrice due to Her Gender, Gender Discrimination still Serious], *China Youth Daily*, November 17, 2014, http://www.chinanews.com/edu/2014/11-17/6781775.shtml

6. Wang Haiyan. "对媒体商业化环境下'新闻业女性化'的质疑," [Questioning 'the Feminization of the News Industry' in the Commercialized Media Environment], *Shanghai Journalism Review*, December 2012, http://journalist.news365.com.cn/tsjw/201212/t20121212_883941.html

7. The Female Journalists Working Committee of the Shanghai Journalists Association. "2013年上海市女性新闻工作者调查报告," [2013 Shanghai Female Journalists Survey], *Shanghai Journalism Review*, May 22, 2014, http://jour.cssn.cn/xwcbx/xwcbx_xwll/201405/t20140522_1180942.shtml

8. Osnos, Evan. "The Forbidden Zone," *The New Yorker*, July 20, 2009. http://www.newyorker.com/magazine/2009/07/20/the-forbidden-zone.

9. Jiang Yiping. "江艺平: 父亲的乌坎," [Jiang Yiping: Father's Wukan], *Caijing*, October 14, 2013,http://www.21ccom.net/articles/rwcq/article_2013101493597.html

10. Svensson, Marina, Elin Saether and Zhi'an Zhang. *Chinese Investigative Journalists' Dreams*. Lanham, MD: Lexington Books, 2014.

11. Ibid., 6.

12. Ibid., 10.

13. http://news.qq.com/a/20120529/000677.htm.

14. Porter, Tom. "Chinese Secret Police Chief Zhou Yongkang Used State TV 'Like Harem,'" *International Business Times*, February 16, 2014, http://www.ibtimes.co.uk/former-chinese-secret-police-chief-zhou-yongkang-used-state-tv-like-harem-1436660.

Index